David Sawtell is at 39 Essex Chambers. He was called to the Bar by Lincoln's Inn in 2005. His practice combines property law, construction law and commercial work, both domestically and internationally. He undertook his BA and his MPhil at the University of Cambridge, and completed the MSc in Construction Law at King's College, London. David is a Fellow of the Chartered Institute of Arbitrators. He is currently researching towards his PhD at the University of Cambridge.

Damian Falkowski is in independent practice as a barrister, having been called to the Bar by Gray's Inn in 1994. He has been a Bencher of Gray's Inn since 2008. Damian undertakes litigation and advisory work in all aspects of the law of real property. His commercial practice includes banking, charges and guarantees, consumer credit, financial regulation, trading platforms and blockchain.

A Practical Guide to the Landlord and Tenant Act 1954: Commercial Tenancies

2nd Edition

A Practical Guide to the Landlord and Tenant Act 1954: Commercial Tenancies

2nd Edition

David Sawtell
Barrister at Law, 39 Essex Chambers,
MA (Cantab), MPhil (Cantab), MSc (KCL), FCIArb

Damian Falkowski
Bencher of Gray's Inn,
A.R.C.M., B.Mus., M.Mus., L.L.Dip.

Law Brief Publishing

Published 2021 by Law Brief Publishing, an imprint of Law Brief Publishing Ltd
30 The Parks
Minehead
Somerset
TA24 8BT

www.lawbriefpublishing.com

Paperback: 978-1-914608-10-0

For Elizabeth, my wife for her continuing support and devotion, and for Michaella, whose guidance and discussions on the 1954 Act led in no little part to the beginning of this project.

(DS)

And

For my wife, Rosalind and daughter Clara.

(DF)

We would also like to give especial thanks to (now District Judge) Richard Hayes, who was the co-author with David of the First Edition of this book. His words substantially remain intact in this Second Edition, which is a tribute to the lucidity and learning in his writing, as well as to the overall stability of this vintage legislation.

CONTENTS

Chapter One	Introduction	1
Chapter Two	Tenancies Which Are Protected by the LTA 1954	5
Chapter Three	Contracting Out of the LTA 1954	27
Chapter Four	Service of Notices, and Obtaining Necessary Information	35
Chapter Five	Security of Tenure Under the LTA 1954	43
Chapter Six	Forfeiture of a Tenancy Under the LTA 1954	47
Chapter Seven	Other Methods of Termination: Disclaimer, Merger and Frustration	59
Chapter Eight	Tenant's Application for a New Tenancy	65
Chapter Nine	Tenant's Termination of a Tenancy	73
Chapter Ten	Landlord's Notice to Terminate a Tenancy	77
Chapter Eleven	The Grounds of Opposition to the Grant of a New Lease to the Tenant	91
Chapter Twelve	Ground A – Tenant's Disrepair	97
Chapter Thirteen	Ground B – Persistent Delay in Paying Rent	103
Chapter Fourteen	Ground C – Tenant's Substantial Breaches	105
Chapter Fifteen	Ground D – Suitable Alternative Accommodation	107

Chapter Sixteen	Ground E – Subletting	111
Chapter Seventeen	Ground F – Landlord Intends to Demolish or Reconstruct the Premises	113
Chapter Eighteen	Ground G – Landlord Intends to Occupy the Holding	129
Chapter Nineteen	Compensation for No-Fault Termination	139
Chapter Twenty	Interim Continuation and Interim Rent	145
Chapter Twenty-One	Deciding the Terms of the New Tenancy	151
Chapter Twenty-Two	Compensation for Improvements Under the Landlord and Tenant Act 1927 and Dilapidations	161
Chapter Twenty-Three	Court Procedure	171
Chapter Twenty-Four	Conclusion: The Future of the LTA 1954	189
Appendix	Notices Under the Landlord and Tenant Act 1954	193

CHAPTER ONE
INTRODUCTION

"L'Anglettere est une nation de boutiquiers"
– as commonly attributed to Napoleon Bonaparte

The Landlord and Tenant Act 1954 ('LTA 1954' or 'the Act') is probably the most important piece of legislation on the statute book concerning premises occupied for business purposes.

If you drive down any high street in this nation of shopkeepers it is likely that you will pass numerous sets of premises to which the Act applies.

The full workings of the Act will be developed over the coming chapters but a thumbnail simplified overview of how it operates is as follows:

- Part II of the Act confers security of tenure upon certain business tenancies so that they do not come to an end at the contractual term date; instead, provided that the tenancy contains premises which are occupied by the tenant for business purposes at term date, the tenancy is continued by statutory magic until terminated in accordance with the Act's provisions.

- The tenant under such a tenancy has the right, on taking certain steps in accordance with the Act, to a new tenancy of the occupied premises, unless the landlord can demonstrate a ground of opposition under section 30(1) of the Act; the old tenancy is continued in the interim.

- In relation to certain grounds of opposition, if the ground is made out the tenant is entitled to statutory compensation on vacating the premises.

- If a new tenancy is granted it can be up-to 15 years, will be at market rent (subject to certain 'disregards') and on terms agreed by the parties or, in default of agreement, set by the court.

- Generally speaking, either the landlord or the tenant can set in motion the machinery that leads to the court deciding whether there should be a new tenancy or not.

- Certain common law methods of termination are preserved, *e.g.* forfeiture, surrender and notice to quit served by the tenant.

- By a defined procedure within LTA 1954 and the regulations made thereunder the parties may contract out of Part II.

Whilst there has been a great deal of statutory regulation of the residential landlord and tenant sector over the years (the high point, or low point, depending on the reader's perspective, being the Rent Act 1977), there has been relatively little intervention in relation to business tenancies. The LTA 1954 is a notable exception.

Without the protection afforded by Part II, a business tenant would be entirely at the landlord's mercy in attempting to agree a renewal: either accept the landlord's terms (if the landlord is prepared to grant a renewal) or risk losing the goodwill referable to the demised premises. By giving a right to renewal, subject to certain grounds of opposition, the Act seeks to balance the tenant's interests – *i.e.* to goodwill and the non-disturbance of the business – against the landlord's legitimate interests in its premises.

The purpose of this text is to provide a practical guide to the workings of the Act.

Definitions

We gather here some definitions that are used with regularity throughout the text:

"**LTA 1954**" means Part II of the Landlord and Tenant Act 1954

"**The Act**" also means Part II of the Landlord and Tenant Act 1954, unless the context suggests otherwise.

"**The 2003 Order**" means the Regulatory Reform (Business Tenancies) (England and Wales) Order 2003.

"**The CPR**" means the Civil Procedure Rules.

"**Section 26 Notice**" means a notice pursuant to that section of LTA 1954, being a notice by which the tenant requests a new tenancy.

"**Section 25 Notice**" means a notice pursuant to that section of the LTA 1954 by which the Landlord seeks to terminate the existing tenancy and either (a) signals that it will oppose the grant of a new tenancy ("**a Hostile Section 25 Notice**") or (b) signals that it is prepared to grant a new tenancy ("**a Non-Hostile Section 25 notice**").

We also adopt the common convention in practice of referring to the various bases of landlord opposition set out in section 30 (1) (a) –(g) LTA 1954 as "**Grounds**".

Structure

In Chapter 2 we look at the tenancies to which the Act applies. Certain tenancies are contracted out of Part II protection: we consider these in Chapter 3. Chapter 4 considers services of notices under the LTA 1954. Chapter 5 describes the means by which a tenancy continues under the Act. Chapters 6 and 7 address other methods of termination preserved by LTA 1954. We then turn to claims for a new tenancy (or by a landlord for termination of the continuation tenancy without the grant of a new tenancy). The tenant's application for a new tenancy is the subject of Chapter 8, and Chapters 9 and 10 deal with termination. Chapters 11 through to 18 discuss in detail the various bases on which a landlord can seek to resist the tenant's claim for a new tenancy, or seek termination. In certain circumstances a tenant which is refused a new tenancy will be entitled to statutory compensation: we explore this in Chapter 19. Chapter 20 addresses the important interim rent provisions within the Act. Chapter 21 contains treatment of the approach the court takes to deciding the terms of a new tenancy. Chapter 22 addresses entitlement to compensation for improvements, and some pointers as regards dilapidations. Chapter 23 deals with the procedure rules under the CPR and our concluding thoughts are in Chapter 24.

Changes since the 1st Edition

Since the 1st Edition, one of the original authors, Richard Hayes, has been elevated to the District Judge bench. David Sawtell has been joined by Damian Falkowksi. Richard's stamp on the text remains in this book, however, and the current authors are grateful to him for his contribution to the success of the original edition.

In the four years since the 1st Edition, the major development in this area was the Supreme Court decision in *S Franses Ltd v Cavendish Hotel (London) Ltd* [2018] UKSC 62, which re-shaped our understanding of the meaning of intention in Ground F and Ground G cases. This 2nd Edition reflects the impact of this case. It does not attempt to deal with cases under the Electronic Communications Code 2017 except in passing. In updating this book, the aim of the authors has been to maintain the structure and clarity of the 1st Edition, rather than adding new material where it does not assist what is intended to be a practical guide. There have, however, been a number of developments in the law of forfeiture, which are reflected in Chapter 6.

From March 2020, England and Wales saw a number of emergency measures enacted as part of the response to the COVID-19 pandemic. In particular, business tenants were protected from eviction by section 82 of the Coronavirus Act 2020 and by second legislation. At the time of writing, some of these enactments remained in force: in particular, the relevant period for the purpose of section 82(12) was extended to 30 June 2021 by regulation 2 of the Business Tenancies (Protection from Forfeiture: Relevant Period) (Coronavirus) (England) Regulations 2021 (SI 2021/283). This book does not intend to deal with these temporary provisions, and the reader's attention is drawn to the UK government's website for up-to-date information. The law is stated as at 30th June 2021.

David Sawtell
39 Essex Chambers

Damian Falkowski
Bencher of Gray's Inn

With thanks to Richard Hayes, co-author of the First Edition

CHAPTER TWO

TENANCIES WHICH ARE PROTECTED BY THE LTA 1954

Section 23(1) LTA 1954 states that 'Subject to the provisions of this Act, this Part of this Act applies to any tenancy where the property comprised in the tenancy is or includes premises which are occupied by the tenant and are so occupied for the purposes of a business carried on by him or for those and other purposes'. The starting point is simple: all business tenancies are protected by the LTA 1954 unless something takes them outside its protection.

Section 23(1) can be broken down as follows:

- <u>There must be a tenancy</u>. Licences as well as tenancies at will fall outside the protection of the LTA 1954. This can lead to difficulties where an occupier has possession of a property and pays a periodic sum as consideration for that occupation: is it a lease or a licence?

- <u>The tenant must occupy premises within the property that is comprised in the tenancy.</u> It is possible for a tenant to cease occupation, or to cease its business in the property, and then for it to lose the benefit of protection under the LTA 1954.

- <u>The tenant's occupation is for the purposes of a business</u>. The LTA 1954 has been interpreted so that 'business' is given a very broad definition. For example, it can include charitable or religious use.

- <u>The business must be carried on by him</u>. This is broadened by a number of statutory provisions to include companies related to the tenant.

Each of these different elements, plus exclusions to the LTA 1954, are discussed below.

What is a 'tenancy'?

The word 'tenancy' means a normal leasehold relationship, including a sublease.

Section 69(1) LTA 1954 gives a full interpretation of the meaning of the word within Part II:

> *"tenancy" means a tenancy created either immediately or derivatively out of the freehold, whether by a lease or underlease, by an agreement for a lease or underlease or by a tenancy agreement or in pursuance of any enactment (including this Act), but does not include a mortgage term or any interest arising in favour of a mortgagor by his attorning tenant to his mortgagee, and references to the granting of a tenancy and to demised property shall be construed accordingly*

Ordinary landlord and tenant principles are applied to distinguish between a licensee (who is not protected by the LTA 1954) and a tenant (who is capable of being protected). In *Street v Mountford* [1985] AC 809 it was held that an agreement granting exclusive occupation of residential accommodation for a term at a rent (where no services are provided), where the grantor was providing neither attendance nor services, creates a tenancy, notwithstanding the use of the word 'licence'. The position is the same whether one is looking at occupation of a residential property or at occupation of a commercial property: *London & Associated Investment Trust Plc v Calow* [1986] 2 EGLR 80. A draftsman of a licence needs to be careful to ensure that a tenancy is not inadvertently granted which is then not contracted out of the LTA 1954. It is the true substance of the relationship that will determine whether the relationship is really one of licence or tenancy.

A genuine tenancy on sufferance or a tenancy at will is also excluded from statutory protection: *Wheeler v Mercer* [1957] AC 416. Although an express agreement for a tenancy at will falls outside the protection of the LTA 1954 the court will consider the reality of the situation applying normal *Street v Mountford* principles.

What are 'premises which are occupied'?

The term 'premises' acquires an important meaning in the LTA 1954. The subject matter of the tenancy must be property which is capable of being occupied. For example, a lease of an easement does not, by itself, attract the protection of the Act, unless it is property that it is actually possible to occupy.

In *Land Reclamation Co. Ltd v Basildon District Council* [1979] 1 WLR 767 the tenant had a tenancy of a right of way along a private road which it used exclusively for business purposes. It was held that the right of way was not protected by the LTA 1954 as an easement (by itself) could not be 'occupied'. The Court of Appeal referred to *Stumbles v Whitley* [1930] AC 544, which was a case under the Landlord and Tenant Act 1927, where it was held that fishing rights were not 'premises', although the tenant was able to obtain a grant of such rights as part of the grant of a new lease of a hotel.

An easement of a car parking space can, however, be occupied, if the right conferred on the tenant was to the effect of excluding the landlord, and hence falls within the LTA 1954: *Pointon York Group v Poulton* [2006] 3 EGLR 37.

Land Reclamation was considered by the Court of Appeal in *Nevill Long & Co (Boards) Ltd and another v Firmenich & Co* [1983] 2 EGLR 76. In that case, there had been a severance of the reversions so that the rights of way that were part of the business lease now passed over land that was owned by a different freehold owner. It was held that the severance of the reversions did not create a separate tenancy in respect of each severed part of the reversion as a consequence of the provisions of section 140(1) Law of Property Act 1925. Notwithstanding the severance of the reversions, there continued in existence under each of the leases a single tenancy of the property thereby demised including the right of way. As in each lease the actual land was occupied for the purpose of the lessee's business, each such tenancy was within section 23. The problem of split reversions for the landlord when serving a section 25 notice is discussed in Chapter 10.

As for occupation itself, this is a matter of fact, giving the words their ordinary meaning. In *Graysim Holdings Ltd Respondent v P. & O. Property*

Holdings Ltd [1996] AC 329 Lord Nicholls held at 334 that the concept of occupation is not a legal term of art, with one single and precise legal meaning applicable in all circumstances. However, the LTA 1954 does not allow for two persons (such as the tenant and a subtenant), other than persons acting jointly, being in occupation of the same property for the purpose of the legislation. In *Bagettes Ltd v G.P. Estates Ltd* [1956] Ch 290, the tenant sublet unfurnished residential flats for business purposes: the Court of Appeal held that the common parts then fell outside the LTA 1954 as once the flats were gone, the business for the purpose of which the tenant occupied the retained parts was also gone. See also the section below on the definition of 'holding'.

On the other hand, some businesses, such as hotels and storage units, are in the business of providing accommodation or space: the business owner is still in occupation. If the landlord's use of the retained parts is merely ancillary to the subtenants' use of their units, providing access and facilities, it is difficult to see how the tenant has 'retained' occupation for the purpose of the LTA 1954. The extent of presence by the tenant required to fall within the protection of the LTA 1954 is a matter of fact and degree.

It is possible for a tenant to occupy premises through an agent or manager: *Parkes v Westminster Roman Catholic Diocese Trustee* (1978) 36 P & CR 22.

What is a 'business'?

Section 23(2) states that, in Part II of the LTA 1954, the expression 'business' includes 'a trade, profession or employment and includes any activity carried on by a body of persons, whether corporate or unincorporate.'

On the other hand, the subletting of parts of premises as flats with a view to making a profit from the rentals is not a business in respect of which the person carrying it on is entitled to security of tenure under the LTA 1954: *Bagettes Ltd v. G.P. Estates Ltd* [1956] Ch 290. In *Trans-Britannia Properties v Darby Properties* [1986] 1 EGLR 151 it was noted that even if the majority of the premises are sub-let, so at first blush it might appear difficult for the lessee to assert that they are in occupation of the site, the court needs to consider the degree of control and extent of the services provided by the tenant company.

This definition includes 'businesses' whose affairs are not strictly profit-making: for example, see *Hawkesbrook Leisure Ltd v Reece-Jones Partnership* [2004] 2 EGLR 61, a case where sports grounds were managed with a view to making a profit or surplus, albeit not distributable to members or shareholders, and the business was carried on as a trading activity. In *Parkes v Westminster Roman Catholic Diocese Trustee* (1978) 36 P & CR 22, the Court of Appeal confirmed that the provision and running of a community centre run by the local parish priest was a 'business.' Lord Denning MR analysed the legal structure of the Roman Catholic Church, noting that it had a structure which is very common to charitable organisations. A body of trustees (which, in this case, was a company limited by guarantee) held the legal title in the property and all of the assets. The trustees were given power by a trust deed to hold property and to use and apply it as capital and income. To the Court of Appeal, the activities of the Church were quite clearly a 'business' for the purpose of section 23(2) LTA 1954. Bridge LJ went so far as to confirm that '"Business" of course is extremely widely defined in the Act as including any activity-carried on by a body of persons corporate or unincorporate.' In *Ruby Triangle Properties Ltd v Jesus Sanctuary Ministries Ltd* [2020] EWHC 2247 (Ch) it was conceded that an evangelical church was a business for the purpose of 23(2) LTA 1954 and that the rental agreement in question amounted to a tenancy as opposed to a licence.

In *Panton v Brophy* [2019] EWHC 1534 (Ch), Master Clark considered whether or not the unincorporated association constituting the famous Thames Tradesmen's Rowing Club constituted a 'business': it was held that it was (at [95]).

A property can be occupied for the purpose of a business even if it is not used for business activity itself or if is ancillary to the business, such as a store room, a car park or a parking space. This line does have limits however: in *Hillil Property & Investment Co Ltd v Naraine Pharmacy Ltd* (1979) 39 P & CR 67, the tenant owned two adjoining shops, and used one of the shops as a dumping ground for waste materials from other shops. It was held that an activity within section 23(2) must be at least something correlative to the conceptions of 'trade, profession or employment,' rather than a casual operation, and therefore this use fell outside the LTA 1954. This is, however, a question of fact and degree.

Companies and businesses

The business must be carried on by the tenant. This is subject to a number of statutory provisions that broaden and explain this phrase.

Section 23(1A) broadens the definition of 'the carrying on of a business'. Where:

a) a company in which a tenant has a controlling interest in a company which is in occupation or carries on a business, or;

b) where the tenant itself is a company and the person with a controlling interest in the company is the occupier or carries on the business;

their occupation of the premises or carrying on of the business is equated with the tenant. This equivalency is extended throughout Part II of the LTA 1954 by subsection 23(1B).

A tenant can conduct business in a partnership. Goulding J held *In re Crowhurst Park* [1974] 1 WLR 583 that the carrying on of a business by the defendant in partnership with his wife was a carrying on of a business by the defendant himself.

If, however, the tenant sublets the property to a company that they control, and that company carries on business in the demised premises, section 23(1A) will not assist the tenant. In *Smyth-Tyrrell v Bowden* [2018] EWHC 106 (Ch), [2018] 2 P & CR D12, it was held that, by virtue of the subtenancy, the company was carrying out business on the company's property, and not the tenant's.

Premises that cease to be occupied

A tenancy for a fixed term cannot be continued under section 24(1) unless, immediately before the term would at common law expire by effluxion of time, the tenancy is one to which the Act applies: *Esselte v Pearl Assurance* [1997] 1 WLR 891, CA. If the tenant vacates the property before the contractual term date the tenancy will not be one to which Part II of the LTA 1954 applies and it will come to an end, even if the tenant has already applied to the court for the grant of a new tenancy. This means that he or she does not need to serve notice under section 27. This is confirmed in section 27(1A):

> *(1A) Section 24 of this Act shall not have effect in relation to a tenancy for a term of years certain where the tenant is not in occupation of the property comprised in the tenancy at the time when, apart from this Act, the tenancy would come to an end by effluxion of time.*

The question of whether a property 'ceases' to be occupied was explored in *Aspinall Finance Ltd v Viscount Chelsea* [1989] 1 EGLR 103. The mere fact that the tenant is not occupying at the relevant date is not conclusive. Tenants do not have to occupy and carry on business for every hour of every day. Some breaks are inevitable. For example, some businesses that are only open in the summer months and are closed throughout all the winter months; alternatively, there may be a need for urgent structural repairs and the tenants had to go out of physical occupation in order to enable them to be effected. The test is whether the thread of continuity of business user continues or whether it has been broken: *I&H Caplan Ltd v Caplan (No 2)* [1963] 1 WLR 1247. The court will look at whether the tenant has an intention to resume occupancy, although this by itself is probably insufficient. Other, non-conclusive, factors include the time that the business has not been carried on, the intention to resume and the reason why the business is not being carried on, whether the reasons were forced on the tenant, and whether the tenant voluntarily went out.

The holding

Part II of the LTA 1954 uses a term that is infrequently used outside the context of the Act. The term 'the holding' is defined in section 23(3) to mean:

- the property comprised in the tenancy;

- excluding any part of the property which is occupied neither:
    a) by the tenant nor
    b) employed by the tenant,

and employed for the purpose of a business by reason of which the LTA 1954 applies.

If a tenant were to occupy only a part of the demised area (for example, if they have sublet), the holding would only include the part that is occupied by their business. This can have important consequences in a lease renewal case. The holding does not include a part of the property which is not occupied at all.

The distinction is important when it comes to the difference between the automatic security of tenure and the right to a grant of a new lease. As will be explored below, section 24 LTA 1954 gives security of tenure to the 'tenancy' (section 24(1): see above). On the other hand, section 32(1) states that an order for the grant of a new tenancy by the court 'shall be an order for the grant of a new tenancy of the holding; and in the absence of agreement between the landlord and the tenant as to the property which constitutes the holding the court shall in the order designate that property by reference to the circumstances existing at the date of the order.'

Where the tenant has sublet only part of the demised property, for example, the entire tenancy (and hence the property in the part which has been sublet) will continue past the term date of the tenancy by virtue of section 24; but, on an application by either the tenant or the landlord for a new tenancy and upon the court's order for a new tenancy coming into effect this continuation will cease and the new tenancy will consist only of the tenant's holding: section 32(1) LTA 1954 ('an order under section twenty-nine of this Act for the grant of a new tenancy shall be an order for the grant of a new tenancy of the holding; and in the absence of agreement between the landlord and the tenant as to the property which constitutes the holding the court shall in the order designate that property by reference to the circumstances existing at the date of the order'.) The landlord can, however, require the whole of the property in the current tenancy to be included: LTA 1954, section 32(2).

The tenant's motive for occupying the property, turning it into the holding, is not relevant. In *Narcissi v Wolfe* [1960] Ch 10 the subtenant left the premises. The tenant then went into occupation of the parts that had been vacated for the purpose of obtaining a new lease of the whole demise. Roxburgh J held that it was not the Court's business to investigate the tenant's purpose: all that the Court had to investigate was whether there was a real occupation or whether it was simply colourable.

Use of the tenancy for business purposes in breach of covenant

Where a tenant occupies a property and conducts a business there in breach of a prohibition in general terms, applying to the whole of the demised premises, against use for business or for trade or for any profession or employment, the tenancy is not protected by the LTA 1954: see *The Trustees of the Methodist Secondary Schools Trust Deed v O'Leary* (1993) 25 HLR 364. It is important for the landlord to ensure that if there is such a breach that it is not acquiescing in it. On the other hand, a business carried on in breach of covenant prohibiting particular trades or businesses does qualify under the LTA 1954.

Working from home and home businesses

Where employees of the tenant are in occupation of living accommodation, the tenant may nevertheless be in occupation for the purposes of the business if it is necessary for the individual to live in the house in order to perform his duties properly, though not if his occupation is for mere convenience: *Chapman v Freeman* [1978] 1 WLR 1298. In that case, the occupation of a cottage by hotel staff was not necessary for the furtherance of the business, but was merely for the convenience of the business, and therefore was not covered by the LTA 1954. Denning LJ contrasted this with 'the toll-keeper who had to live in a cottage next to the toll-bridge, or the stockman who has to live in the centre of the stockyard so as to carry out his duties. Those servants occupied for the purposes of the business: see *Ramsbottom v Snelson* [1948] 1 KB 473'.

Residential property may in certain circumstances be occupied for the purposes of a business, where the business activity is a significant purpose for the tenant in occupation (where a professional man takes a tenancy of one house for the very purpose of carrying on his profession in one room and of residing in the rest of the house with his family, like the doctor who has a consulting room in his house), as opposed to being purely incidental to his residential occupation (for example, if he incidentally does some work at home): *Cheryl Investments Ltd. v. Saldanha* [1978] 1 WLR 1329.

The 'home worker' who decides to give up his office and to do all his or her work from his home is now governed by a separate regime. In *Cheryl Investments Ltd*, it was held that this would take him or her into the LTA 1954 regime. This is now significantly altered by a new regime that dates from 2015.

Section 35 of the Small Business, Enterprise and Employment Act 2015 inserted provisions into the LTA 1954 to remove 'home businesses' from the protection of the LTA 1954. These provisions came into force on 1 October 2015 and are subject to a transitional provision at subsection 35(5) of the 2015 Act. The new home business provisions do not apply to:

a) a tenancy which is entered into before 1 October 2015;

b) a tenancy which is entered into on or after 1 October 2015, pursuant to a contract made before that day;

c) a tenancy which arises by operation of any enactment or other law when a tenancy mentioned in paragraph (a) or (b) comes to an end.

Subsection 5 now contains a convoluted provision in respect of home businesses. These are defined in section 43ZA. Subsection 43ZA(1) confirms that Part II of the LTA 1954 does not apply to a 'home business tenancy'. Subsection 43ZA(4) states that a 'home business' is a business of a kind which might reasonably be carried on at home'. Subsection 5 (presumably to protect public houses) states that 'A business is not to be treated as a home business if it involves the supply of alcohol for consumption on licensed premises which form all or part of the dwelling-house'.

Subsection 43ZA(2) defines a home business tenancy as a tenancy under which:

a) a dwelling-house is let as a separate dwelling,

b) the tenant or, where there are joint tenants, each of them, is an individual, and

c) the terms of the tenancy—

    a. require the tenant or, where there are joint tenants, at least one of them, to occupy the dwelling-house as a home (whether or not as that individual's only or principal home),

    b. permit a home business to be carried on in the dwelling-house, or permit the immediate landlord to give consent for a home business to be carried on in the dwelling-house, and

    c. do not permit a business other than a home business to be carried on in the dwelling-house.

Section 41(3) states that where a tenancy is held on trust, section 43ZA(2) is modified: paragraph (b) (the requirement that the tenant or joint tenants is an individual) is omitted, and the condition that the terms of the tenancy require the tenant(s) to occupy the dwelling-house as a home is altered, so that it is a condition that the terms of the tenancy require at least one individual who is a trustee or a beneficiary under the trust to occupy the dwelling-house as a home.

Subsection 43ZA(9) provides that if, under a tenancy, a dwelling-house is let together with other land, then, for the purposes of the home business provisions:

a) if the main purpose of the letting is the provision of a home for the tenant, the other land is to be treated as part of the dwelling-house, and

b) if this is not the main purpose of the letting, the tenancy is to be treated as not being one under which a dwelling-house is let as a separate dwelling.

Where the tenant's breach of a prohibition of use for business purposes is one of the terms of the tenancy, this prohibition extends to the whole of the property, and the breach itself consists 'solely of carrying on a home business', Part II of the LTA 1954 will not apply: section 23(5) LTA 1954. This is the case even if the immediate landlord or the immediate landlord's predecessor in title has consented to the breach, or if the immediate landlord has acquiesced in the breach. This is a sharp distinction from the normal situation discussed above, where consent to or waiver of the breach could bring the tenancy under the Act's protection.

Other excluded leases

Section 43 contains provisions excluding a list of other types of tenancies from the protection of the LTA 1954. These are:

a) a tenancy of an agricultural holding which is a tenancy in relation to which the Agricultural Holdings Act 1986 applies, or a tenancy which would be a tenancy of an agricultural holding in relation to which that Act applied if subsection (3) of section 2 of that Act did not have effect or, in a case where approval was given under subsection (1) of that section, if that approval had not been given (subsection (1)(a));

b) a farm business tenancy (subsection (1)(aa));

c) a tenancy created by a mining lease (subsection 1(b));

d) a tenancy granted by reason that the tenant was the holder of an office, appointment or employment from the grantor thereof, and continuing only so long as the tenant holds the office, appointment or employment, or terminable by the grantor on the tenant's ceasing to hold it, or coming to an end at a time fixed by reference to the time at which the tenant ceases to hold it (although this subsection does not effect to a tenancy granted after the commencement of the LTA 1954 unless the tenancy was granted by an instrument in writing which expressed the purpose for which the tenancy was granted) (subsection (2)).

Under section 43(3), Part II of the LTA 1954 also does not apply to shorter leases except in certain circumstances. It does not apply to a tenancy granted for a term certain not exceeding six months unless:

a) the tenancy contains provision for renewing the term or for extending it beyond six months from its beginning; or

b) the tenant has been in occupation for a period which, together with any period during which any predecessor in the carrying on of the business carried on by the tenant was in occupation, exceeds twelve months.

Contracting out of the LTA 1954

It is possible to contract out of the provisions of Part II of the LTA 1954. This is the most important way a business tenancy falls outside the protection of the Act. Contracting out is discussed in Chapter 3.

The inadvertent creation and inheritance of LTA 1954 protected tenancies

Tenancy granted instead of a licence

As discussed above, the LTA 1954 does not apply to a licence but does apply to a tenancy, whatever the description of the form of occupation given by the parties. An example of this is *Mann Aviation Group (Engineering) Ltd v Longmint Aviation Ltd and another* [2011] EWHC 2238 (Ch). The tenant, MAGE, designed and constructed small aircraft and helicopters in aircraft hangars and storage buildings. When it went into administration, the administrators claimed that they had the benefit of an implied periodic tenancy. Longmint, the owner of a 10-year lease in respect of these buildings, denied this, and averred that they were a mere licensee. Sale J, applying *Street v Mountford*, noted that MAGE had the power to exclude persons from their premises. The sum paid for occupation was described as rent. Even though there was not a written tenancy agreement, the circumstances showed that the parties intended to enter into a relationship of landlord and tenant. As it was a periodic tenancy it was an overriding interest that was thus binding on Longmint. As it had not been contracted out of the LTA 1954, it was protected by the Act.

Another example is *London College of Business Limited v Tareem Limited* [2018] EWHC 437 (Ch), where it was held that a lease had been created between the parties despite the plain wording of the 'licence agreement'. The purpose of the agreement was to provide the College with premises from which it could conduct its educational business; it was not realistic to suppose that the parties genuinely intended that the College's business could be interrupted by the 'licensor's' right to enter the units occupied by the college, not that the 'licensor' had any genuine commercial interest in doing so: 'In substance, if not in form, the clear intent was that the College should be allowed to get on with running its business provided that it paid the stipulated amount.' The agreement did not reflect the reality of the situation. As a consequence, the tenant had a tenancy, which was a business tenancy for the purpose of Part II of the LTA 1954. As Lord Templeman said in *Street v Mountford* [1985] A.C. 809: 'The manufacture of a five pronged implement for manual digging results in a fork even if the manufacturer, unfamiliar with the English language, insists that he intended to make and has made a spade.'

Subletting

A sub-tenancy is a tenancy under section 69 LTA 1954. Whether or not your direct tenant is in breach of covenant by subletting, if they themselves have not taken adequate precautions it is possible that a sublease may fall within the LTA 1954. If the client then evicts the direct tenant the sublease will remain, leaving him or her as their direct landlord: *D'Silva v Lister House Development* [1971] Ch 17. The superior landlord might still be able to rely on forfeiture. Furthermore, the unlawful grant of a sublease might allow the landlord to oppose the grant of a new lease to both the tenant and the subtenant under section 30(1)(c).

Although unlawful subletting might potentially be a ground for forfeiture, the landlord must be careful to ensure that if he or she does intend to forfeit (and hence destroy the sub-tenancy) and the tenant has demised the whole of the property, that the forfeiture takes place before the tenancy expires by effluxion of time. If the landlord waits, the original tenancy will expire so that there will be nothing to forfeit, leaving only the protected sub-tenancy.

Holding over

If a tenant holds over at the end of a fixed term and the parties do not start to negotiate new terms, it is technically possible that a court would hold that they have entered into a new periodic tenancy. As the parties would not have contracted out of the LTA 1954, this new tenancy would be protected: A tenancy at will, however, does not fall under the protection of the LTA 1954: *Wheeler v. Mercer* [1957] AC 416.

This scenario has been considered by the Court of Appeal in two particular cases, namely *Javid v Aqil* [1991] 1 WLR 1007 and *Erimus Housing Ltd v Barclays Wealth Trustees (Jersey) Ltd & Others* [2014] 2 P & CR 85. In *Javid*, the proposed tenant was allowed into the property having paid 'rent for three months in advance' in anticipation that the parties would be able to agree the terms of a lease. No lease was executed and the tenant occasionally paid rent. The parties failed to reach agreement and the landlord sought possession of the property. The Court of Appeal rejected the argument that proof of possession and payment of rent by reference to a quarterly period raises a presumption in favour of a periodic tenancy which can only be rebutted by an express agreement. It was held that, as a matter of principle, a tenancy springs from a consensual arrangement between two parties: the extent of the right granted and accepted depends primarily upon the intention of the parties. The law will imply, from what was agreed and all the surrounding circumstances, the terms the parties are to be taken to have intended to apply. While the parties are still negotiating for more than a licence, caution must be exercised before inferring or imputing to the parties an intention to give to the occupant more than a very limited interest.

This decision was confirmed in *Erimus*, where the negotiations were 'desultory and lacking any impetus' [13]. There was, however, no evidence that the negotiations had ceased or been abandoned. At [23] it was again emphasised that holding over and paying rent gave rise to no presumption of a periodic tenancy: instead, 'the parties' contractual intentions fall to be determined by looking objectively at all relevant circumstances', the most significant of which was the ongoing negotiations for a new formal lease. This was contrasted with *Walji v Mount Cook Land Ltd* [2002] 1 P&CR 13 where the parties reached agreement on the terms of a new lease but then did nothing further for years in terms of executing such a lease. At first instance it was held that a periodic tenancy had come into existence; this decision was affirmed on appeal.

Who is the landlord?

The LTA 1954 differentiates between the immediate landlord (who is the tenant's landlord at common law) and the 'competent' landlord. The competent landlord is the only party who can, for example, serve a section 25 notice. The reason for this distinction is that the immediate landlord may have a term that is only a few days longer than the tenant's interest, and hence not be able to grant a new tenancy under the LTA 1954. The situation is complicated where there is an intermediate landlord who has sublet part of their demise to tenant protected by LTA 1954, but who himself or herself also has the protection of the LTA 1954. (If they have sublet the whole of their demise, they are no longer in occupation of the property for the purpose of their business, and therefore are not protected by the LTA 1954).

Section 44(1) LTA 1954 confirms that, in Part II of the LTA 1954, the expression 'the landlord' means 'the person (whether or not he is the immediate landlord) who is the owner of that interest in the property comprised in the relevant tenancy which for the time being fulfils the following conditions', namely:

- it is an interest in reversion expectant (whether immediately or not) on the termination of the relevant tenancy, and

- it is either:

  - the fee simple; or
  - a tenancy which will not come to an end within fourteen months by effluxion of time and, if it is such a tenancy, that no notice has been given by virtue of which it will come to an end within fourteen months or any further time by which it may be continued under section 36(2) or section 64 of this Act; and

- and is not itself in reversion expectant (whether immediately or not) on an interest which fulfils those conditions.

On the other hand, a reference to a 'notice to quit' given by the landlord in the LTA 1954 is a reference to a notice given by the immediate landlord.

Only the competent landlord may serve or receive a section 25 or section 26 notice respectively. A section 27 notice can be served on the immediate landlord.

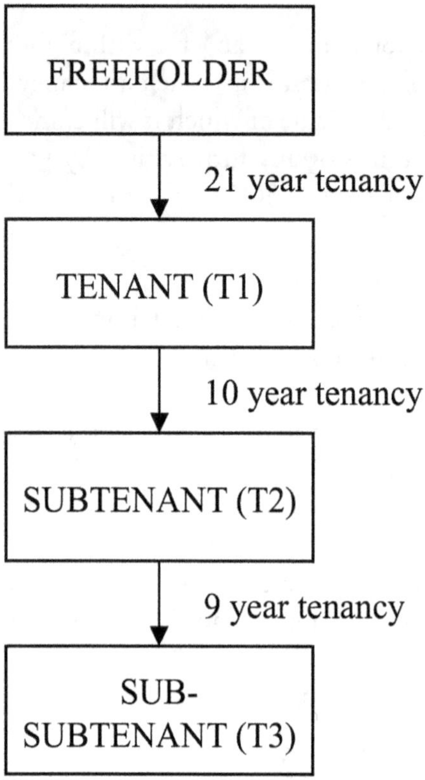

EXAMPLE:

T3's lease (which comprises the whole of the premises) is about to expire. Although T2 is the immediate landlord, its own lease has less than 14 months to run. T1 is therefore the competent landlord.

If, however, T2 had granted only half of the premises to T3 and occupied the other half for its own business premises (so that it is in business occupation), T2's lease will not expire in less than 14 months as it will be continued by section 24(1) and it will not come to an end by effluxion of time. T2 will therefore be T3's competent landlord.

Given this complicated relationship between the tenant, the intermediate landlord (or landlords) and the competent landlord, the LTA 1954 goes into some detail as to the mechanics of how this is given effect. Schedule 6 of the LTA 1954 provides further provisions where the immediate landlord is not the freeholder. Paragraph 1 defines the following terms:

- "the competent landlord" means the person who in relation to the tenancy is for the time being the landlord as defined by section 44 of the LTA 1954;

- "mesne landlord" means a tenant whose interest is intermediate between the relevant tenancy and the interest of the competent landlord;

- "superior landlord" means a person (whether the owner of the fee simple or a tenant) whose interest is superior to the interest of the competent landlord.

What happens if the new tenancy will extend beyond the term of the immediate landlord?

Where, in accordance with the LTA 1954, the period for which it is agreed or determined by the court that a new tenancy should be granted thereunder will extend beyond the date on which the interest of the immediate landlord will come to an end, the power of the court under the Act to order such a grant shall include power to order the grant of a new tenancy until the expiration of that interest and also to order the grant of such a reversionary tenancy or reversionary tenancies as may be required to secure that the combined effects of those grants will be equivalent to the grant of a tenancy for that period (paragraph 2, Schedule 6).

The competent landlord's notices and agreements made binding on intermediate landlords

Paragraph 3(1), Schedule 6 confirms that any notice given by the competent landlord to terminate the relevant tenancy, and any agreement made between that landlord and the tenant as to the granting, duration, or terms of a future tenancy under the LTA 1954, shall bind the interest of any mesne landlord notwithstanding that he has not consented to the giving of the notice or was not a party to the agreement. Further, under para 3(2), the competent landlord shall have power for the purposes of the LTA 1954 to give effect to any agreement with the tenant for the grant of a new tenancy beginning with the coming to an end of the relevant tenancy, notwithstanding that the competent landlord will not be the immediate landlord at the commencement of the new tenancy, and any instrument made in the exercise of the power conferred by para 3(2) shall have effect as if the mesne landlord had been a party.

Compensation where the competent landlord does not obtain consent from intermediate landlords

This power under para 3 is not, however, without liability. Paragraph 4(1), Schedule 6 provides for compensation to be payable by the competent landlord to mesne landlords whose consent has not been given for any loss arising in consequence of the giving of the notice or the making of the agreement.

Consent not to be unreasonably withheld

If the competent landlord applies to any mesne landlord for his consent to such a notice or agreement, that consent shall not be unreasonably withheld, but may be given subject to any conditions which may be reasonable (including conditions as to the modification of the proposed notice or agreement or as to the payment of compensation by the competent landlord) (para 4(2)).

The relationship between the competent landlord and any superior landlord

An agreement between the competent landlord and the tenant made for the purposes of the LTA 1954 in a case where—

a) the competent landlord is himself a tenant, and

b) the agreement would, apart from paragraph 5, operate as respects any period after the coming to an end of the interest of the competent landlord,

shall not have effect unless every superior landlord who will be the immediate landlord of the tenant during any part of that period is a party to the agreement (para 5).

Allied to this provision is para 7. If the competent landlord's interest in the property comprised in the relevant tenancy is a tenancy which will come or can be brought to an end within sixteen months (or any further time by which it may be continued under section 36(2) or section 64 of the LTA 1954) and he or she gives to the tenant under the relevant tenancy a section 25 notice to terminate the tenancy or receives a section 26 notice:

a) the competent landlord shall forthwith send a copy of the notice to his immediate landlord; and

b) any superior landlord whose interest in the property is a tenancy shall forthwith send to his immediate landlord any copy which has been sent to him in pursuance of para 7(a) or 7(b).

The superior landlord may, however, become the competent landlord after a section 25 notice has been served. Where the competent landlord has given a section 25 notice to terminate the relevant tenancy and, within two months after the giving of the notice, a superior landlord:

a) becomes the competent landlord; and

b) gives to the tenant notice in the prescribed form that he withdraws the notice previously given;

the section 25 notice shall cease to have effect, but without prejudice to the giving of a further notice under that section by the competent landlord. (para 6). The prescribed form is form number 7 of the Landlord and Tenant Act 1954, Part 2 (Notices) Regulations 2004 (SI 2004/1005).

CHAPTER THREE
CONTRACTING OUT OF THE LTA 1954

As originally enacted it was not possible for the parties to contract out of sections 24-28 of LTA 1954, being the core provisions of the Act which provide for the continuation of the tenancy and the tenant's right, subject to the Act's terms, to a new tenancy. By amendments effective from 1st January 1970, however, parties were permitted to agree to exclude the operation of those sections in relation to an intended lease, providing that the appropriate statutory procedure was followed.

The procedure was overhauled by the 2003 Order and different rules apply dependent upon whether the agreement in question was entered into prior to 1st June 2004, in which case a court application is necessary, or on/after that date in which case a notice procedure needs to be followed.

Although it is commonly said in practice that parties who follow the appropriate procedures 'contract out of' the Act – or that the lease is 'contracted out' – it is important to keep in mind that the relevant tenancy will still be one to which the LTA 1954 more generally applies, albeit subject to the important exception that sections 24-28 will not apply. The point is not simply a technical nicety as it can be important for other purposes, notably in ascertaining whether various residential codes affording security of tenure apply (for example the Rent Act 1977 or the Housing Act 1988) as the applicability of those residential codes is framed in part by excluding from their reach tenancies to which the LTA 1954 applies. A 'contracted out' tenancy satisfying the requirements for the application of Part II LTA 1954 will, therefore, be outside the protection of those residential codes.

This chapter is confined to agreements to exclude sections 24-28 of the Act (and agreements for surrender); for the separate question of whether, and if so when, the parties can contract out of, or contractually regulate, compensation for disturbance please see Chapter 19.

The general prohibition on contracting out

The general rule is set out in section 38(1) of the Act: any '*...agreement relating to a tenancy to which this Part of this Act applies (whether contained in the instrument creating the tenancy or not) shall be void except as provided by section 38A of this Act in so far as it purports to preclude the tenant from making an application or request under the Part of this Act or provides for the termination or the surrender of the tenancy in the event of his making such an application or request or for the imposition of any penalty of disability on the tenant in that event*'.

The courts appear to take a purposeful approach to the provision. So, in *Joseph v Joseph* [1967] 78, the Court of Appeal considered that '*purports*' meant '*to have as its effect*', rather than giving the words a strictly linguistic narrow meaning.

The exception to the rule: position prior to 1st June 2004

Section 5 of the Law of Property Act 1969 introduced a mechanism ('the Old Mechanism') for the parties to exclude sections 24-38 of LTA 1954. The Old Mechanism was contained in sub-section 38(4) of the Act, which has since been repealed (subject to transitional provisions) by the 2003 Order.

The Old Mechanism will be dealt with briefly as it is increasingly unlikely to arise in practice. In short, in respect of certain types of tenancy, the prospective parties could make an application to the court for authorisation to exclude the operation of sections 24-28 of the Act from the tenancy into which they intended to enter. Providing that authorisation was granted, and the authorisation was properly referred to in the instrument creating the tenancy, the tenancy would be contracted out of sections 24-28. Similar provisions governed the making of agreements to surrender the tenancy. The types of tenancy in relation to which an application could be made are the same as those under the New Procedure, which is dealt with below.

<u>The position post 1st June 2004</u>

The Old Mechanism was considered somewhat cumbersome. In addition, it engaged court time with what was an essentially administrative task. The 2003 Order sought to simplify matters and introduced a new procedure ('the New Procedure') which applies to all agreements to exclude sections 24-28, or agreements for surrender, reached on or after 1st June 2004. The Old Mechanism cannot be used in relation to such agreements.

As with the Old Procedure, only certain types of tenancy can be contracted out of sections 24-28 under the New Procedure. To be a tenancy which is capable of being excluded, the tenancy must be one which will be "*granted for a term of years certain*": section 38A(1) LTA 1954. This would appear to exclude a periodic tenancy even though such tenancies can attract Part II protection. The inclusion within a fixed term of a break clause does not invalidate it from being a '*term of years certain*' for these purposes: see *The Receiver for the Metropolitan Police District v Palacegate Properties Ltd* [2001] Ch 131.

The New Procedure is to be found in section 38A LTA 1954 and schedules 1-4 of the 2003 Order. Section 38A(3) LTA 1954 provides that unless the appropriate procedure is followed, an agreement to exclude section 24-28 LTA 1954 is void. Similarly, section 38A(4) provides that unless the appropriate procedure is followed as regards an agreement for surrender, such an agreement shall be void.

We shall concentrate on the procedure for contracting out of sections 24-28 LTA 1954 as it is more commonly encountered; the procedure relating to surrender (contained in schedule 3 and 4 to the Act) is similar in requiring a type of prescribed notice and declaration procedure.

To validly contract out of section 24-28 LTA 1954 the procedure is as follows (references to 'landlord' and 'tenant' being to '*the persons who will be the landlord and tenant*' in relation to the tenancy in relation to which those sections are being excluded):

a) The landlord must serve on the tenant a notice in the form, or substantially the form, set out in Schedule 1 to the Order, see section 38A(3)(a) LTA 1954. This is a notice which requires the name and address of the tenant and landlord to be entered. The prescribed notice contains text which effectively constitutes a warning (amongst other information) that the lease which is being offered will not enjoy security of tenure and suggests the prospective tenant should not commit to taking the lease without prior professional advice. We shall refer to this notice as 'the Warning Notice' below. The proposed lease itself does not need to be exhibited to or sent with the Warning Notice. Although a notice in '*substantially*' the same form as that scheduled to the Order will suffice, the landlord should not run the risk in this regard and should ensure that a decent precedent is used to avoid argument.

b) Section 38A(2) LTA 1954 provides that the requirements of Schedule 2 of the Order ('Schedule 2') are met. The Warning Notice must be served prior to the tenant entering, or becoming contractually bound to enter into, the tenancy to which the notice applies. Schedule 2 then requires a documented response from the tenant which can be in one of two different forms dependent upon how long prior to entering into (or becoming obliged to enter into) the lease the Warning Notice was served.

c) Providing the Warning Notice is served not less than 14 days before the tenant enters, or becomes bound to enter into the tenancy, then a declaration in the form, or substantially in the form, set out in paragraph 7 of the Schedule 2 will suffice. This can be made by the tenant '*or a person duly authorised by him to do so*'. To avoid arguments as to whether the person making the declaration is '*duly authorised*' it would be worthwhile ensuring, if possible, that the actual tenant makes the declaration. The declaration required by paragraph 7 sets out (amongst other things) the names and addresses of the parties, the fact the Warning Notice has been served and that the tenant has read and accepts the consequences of entering into the agreement (*i.e.* that the proposed lease will not attract security of tenure). It also repeats the warning information required to be set out in the landlord's notice.

d) Again, notwithstanding the fact that paragraph 3 of Schedule 2 only requires a declaration in 'substantially in the form' of that at paragraph 7, the landlord would be well advised to check any declaration made by the tenant (or person authorised by the tenant) and insist on strict compliance; better that than run the risk of a technical argument at a later stage.

e) If the Warning Notice is served less than 14 days prior to the tenant entering into, or becoming contractually bound to enter into, the lease then a *statutory declaration* is required to be made by the tenant, or a person duly authorised by the tenant, in the form, or substantially in the form, of that set out in paragraph 8 Schedule 2. The statutory declaration under paragraph 8 contains the same details as the simple declaration under paragraph 7; the difference is that the statutory declaration attracts an additional degree of formality as it will need to be made before a solicitor or other person authorised to administer oaths. There is, however, no requirement in the Act for the tenant to receive any advice before such a statutory declaration is valid.

f) Whichever route is taken, a reference to the declaration or statutory declaration (as applicable) must be contained in or endorsed on the instrument creating the tenancy, see paragraph 5, Schedule 2. Furthermore, the agreement under section 38A(1) LTA 1954 must be 'contained in or endorsed upon the instrument creating the tenancy', see paragraph 6 Schedule 2.

The courts do not appear to like unnecessarily technical arguments as regards compliance with these procedures; nor, indeed, did they with the Old Mechanism (as an example of the Court of Appeal eschewing an overly technical approach under the Old Mechanism see *Brighton & Hove City Council v Collinson and another* [2004] 2 EGLR 65). In *Chiltern Railway Co Ltd v Patel* [2008] 2 EGLR 33 the landlord had used the (more formal) statutory declaration procedure even though the Warning Notice was served more than 14 days before the tenant entered into, or became bound to enter into, the lease. An argument by the tenant that this invalidated the agreement to exclude sections 24-28 was given short-shrift: the statutory declaration contained the same information required of the simple declaration and the fact the landlord had, by choice, used the more formal declaration did not matter. Indeed, it is common to find that landlords insist on the use of the more formal statutory declaration procedure because it avoids arguments as to precisely when the Warning Notice was served (*i.e.* whether it was served less than 14 days prior to the tenant entering into or becoming obliged to enter into the tenancy). Note, however, that the contrary is not the case: a landlord who leaves service of the Warning Notice so that less than 14 days warning is given is required to use the statutory declaration.

The Court of Appeal also rejected a technical argument as to compliance in *TFS Stores Ltd v Designer Retail Outlet Centres (Mansfield) General Partner Ltd* [2021] EWCA Civ 688. In that case, the landlord's Warning Notice fully complied with the prescribed form, but the one entry on the tenants' declarations ("for a term commencing on ...") did not specify a particular date (e.g. one declaration stated that the lease would be "for a term commencing on a date to be agreed between the parties"). The argument that as a specific date was not identified the declaration was invalid was rejected: the declarations were held to be in the form or substantially in the form prescribed by the legislation. As Arnold LJ said: '*There is no good reason to treat the "for a term commencing on ... " section of the prescribed form of declaration as an examination question which must be correctly answered by the tenant in order for the parties to achieve the contracting out from Part II of the 1954 Act that they have agreed.*"

However, in *Newnham Council v Thomas Van Staden* [2008] EWCA Civ 1414, a case which concerned the Old Mechanism, the definition of 'the term' of the lease was such as to 'include any period of holding over or extension of it whether by statute or at common law or by agreement' with the result that the lease was not contracted out of section 24 to 28 at all, despite a court order from the county court apparently to that effect.

What if the terms of the proposed tenancy change after the Warning Notice has been served (or after the prospective tenant has made the declaration)? Does a fresh notice need to be served? Under the Old Mechanism this question arose in the case of *The Receivers of the Metropolitan Police District v Palacegate Properties Ltd* [2001] Ch 131. A draft lease had been submitted with a joint application to the court (as was then required as the law stood) for authorisation to exclude sections 24-28. The court acceded to the application. Before the lease was executed, its provisions were altered to provide that rent would be payable in advance rather than in arrears. The parties entered into the lease and in due course the tenant argued that the variation of terms from those which had been before the court at the time it authorised exclusion denuded that order of effect. The Court of Appeal took a practical view that the purpose of the regime under the Act was simply to ensure that the tenant understood it was foregoing protection, rather than the court being concerned as to the precise terms of the prospective tenancy. However, the court did take the view that a 'wholesale' departure from the draft terms would have been unacceptable; the eventual terms must bear a substantial similarity to those which had been put before the court. Pill LJ considered that a material change might be one which related, say, to the length of the term, so the inclusion of a break clause might be considered relevant for these purposes. Although there appears no case law as yet under the New Procedure on this point it is likely the court would take a similar view. That said, it would be best not to court controversy or argument: it is therefore suggested that if the proposed terms change and the landlord would be best advised to serve a fresh Warning Notice and seek a new declaration.

CHAPTER FOUR

SERVICE OF NOTICES AND OBTAINING NECESSARY INFORMATION

It will be apparent that the workings of Part II of the LTA 1954 are often dependent on the service of correct notices on (and by) the correct people. In this chapter, we consider certain provisions within the Act which deal with (a) the mechanics of service and (b) requests for, and the obligation to provide, certain information necessary for the proper operation of the Act.

Service

At common law, and absent any contractually agreed provisions for service, a person required to serve (or give) a 'notice' to another person is required to prove it has been received by or come to the attention of the recipient, see *Sun Alliance and London Assurance Co Ltd. v Hayman* [1975] 1 WLR 177 [For an excellent treatment of the service of notices in general see *Property Notices, Validity and Service* by Tom Weekes QC, 3rd Edition]. In that case, Salmon LJ stated: "*According to the ordinary and natural use of English words, giving a notice means causing a notice to be received. Therefore, any requirement in a statute or a contract for the giving of a notice can be complied with only by causing the notice to be actually received unless the context or some statutory or contractual provision otherwise provides…*". This proposition was endorsed by the Supreme Court in *UKI (Kingsway) Ltd v Westminster City Council* [2018] UKSC 67, [2019] 1 WLR 104. Specific statutory provisions are generally designed, not to exclude other methods, but rather to protect the server from the risk of non-delivery ([16]).

It is always important to check the lease carefully for provisions which deal with the mechanics of service, as it is open to the parties to adopt contractual mechanics for the service of notices; these often include deeming provisions both as to the fact and date of service.

Section 66(4) LTA 1954 provides that section 23 of the Landlord and Tenant Act 1927 ('the LTA 1927'), which relates to service of notices, shall apply for the purposes of the LTA 1954. Section 23(1) LTA 1927 provides that any notice, request, demand or other instrument shall be in writing and may be served:

a) on the person on whom it is to be served personally; or

b) by leaving it for him at his last known place of above in England or Wales; or

c) by sending it through the post in a registered letter addressed to him at his last known place of abode; or

d) in the case of a local or public authority of a statutory of public utility company sending it through the post in a registered letter addressed to the secretary or other proper office at the principal office of the authority or company;

e) in the case of a notice to a landlord on any duly authorised agent.

These provisions are extremely useful in practice. Where the provisions are properly utilised service is *deemed* to be properly effected irrespective of whether the notice is actually received at all. The practical effect, therefore, is to entirely shift the risk of non-receipt to the party who is to be served. All the "serving" party need prove is that he has taken the steps required by the 1927 Act, rather than having to prove receipt: *Blunden v Frogmore Investments Ltd* [2003] 2 P & CR 6. It is worth noting that there is no provision in section 23 LTA 1927 corresponding to the 'dead-letter service' provision in section 196(4) of the Law of Property Act 1925; under the latter, if a letter is returned undelivered to the postal operator service is not deemed effective. Under the LTA 1927, however, that is not the case and such a document will be properly served.

An additional advantage of using the LTA 1927 Act provisions is certainty not only as to the fact of service but, also, as to the date of service. In *CA Webber (Transport) Ltd v Network Rail Infrastructure Ltd (Formerly Railtrack plc)* [2004] 1 WLR 320 it was held that service was deemed effective when the serving party entrusted the notice to the Post Office, rather than a later date when it was actually received. Section 7 of the Interpretation Act 1978 does not apply to service under the LTA 1927 (note, by contrast, those provisions *do* apply to other methods of service).

The use of any of the methods of service provided by section 23 LTA 1927 is permissive: the parties are not required to use them, *Galinski v McHugh* (1988) 57 P & CR 359.

Certain additional points are worth noting about the LTA 1927 provisions:

- 'Last known place of abode' is construed liberally. It is not confined to a person's residence but also encompasses their business address, see *Price v West London Investment Building Society Ltd* [1964] 1 WLR 616.

- By section 1 of the Recorded Delivery Service Act 1962, the reference in section 23 LTA 1927 to serving by registered post is extended to include service by recorded delivery.

- The first method of service (*i.e.* personal service) has been held to be inapplicable for service upon a company, see *Stylo Shoes Ltd. v Prices Tailors Ltd* [1960] Ch 396 [In *Property Notices, Validity and Service 3rd Edition* at 6.12, Tom Weekes suggests that personal service on an agent is generally impermissible, referring to *Gate Gourmet Luxembourg IV SARL and another v Morby* [2016] EWHC 74 (Ch), but also noting that the contrary is suggested in *Bottin (International) Investment Ltd v Vensoni Group Plc* [2004] EWCA Civ 1368 at [47] by Peter Gibson LJ and in *Ener-G Holdings plc v Hormell* [2012] EWCA Civ 1059 at [21] by the Master of the Rolls. For a different analysis, see *Reynolds & Clark Renewal of Business Tenancies 5th Edition* at 3-54 in which they suggest that the remarks in *Stylo* were *obiter* and personal service on a company through its agents can be effective]. Given the divergence in the caselaw, it would be best to utilise one of the other heads of service in the LTA 1927 to effect service on a corporate landlord.

- It is not entirely clear whether the 'last known place of abode' provisions import any degree of obligation on the serving party to take steps to ascertain the actual place of abode; see *Levette-Dunn and others v NHS Property Services Ltd* [2016] EWHC 943 (Ch) where such an argument, by analogy with the Civil Procedure Rules as to service, appears to have been unsuccessful because the landlord had specified its address in the lease (and the Judge held that until the landlord communicated a new address to the tenant the contractually specified address was to be taken as the landlord's place of abode).

In addition, section 23(2) LTA 1927 deals with the situation where a landlord has transferred its reversion. Until such time as the tenant has received notice that the person hitherto entitled to the rents and profits (called 'the original landlord' in the sub-section) has ceased to be so entitled, and notice of the name and address of the person who has become so entitled, service or delivery of any notice *etc* on the original landlord is deemed effective against the actual landlord.

Requests for information

The mechanics of the LTA 1954 are such that the landlord will be interested to know: (a) whether its tenant is in occupation of any (and if so which) parts of the premises for the purposes of a business; (b) whether the tenant has sub-let any part of the premises and if so for how long, on what terms and whether any sub-tenancy would be within the LTA 1954; (c) similar information as regards any further under-lettings. The tenant, on the other hand, will be interested to ascertain who satisfies the requirements to be 'the landlord' within the meaning of section 44 (*i.e.* the 'competent landlord' as that person is commonly termed); information as to the length and nature of its landlord's (and any superior landlord's) interests, and what notices (if any) have been served on those parties would is relevant to those matters.

Section 40 LTA 1954 enables a landlord or tenant of business premises to serve a notice in certain defined circumstances to flush out certain information. The provisions were overhauled and improved by changes introduced by the 2003 Order; the position stated below is as amended by that Order.

A person served with such a notice is under a duty to provide the information within 1 month, section 40(5)(a) LTA 1954. Further, if, within 6 months of being served with the request for information the person served becomes aware the information is not, or is no longer, correct there is a duty within 1 month to provide the correct information, section 40(5)(b) LTA 1954. Breach of the duty to provide information is a breach of statutory duty for which a damages claim may be brought, section 40B LTA 1954. Provision is made by section 40A LTA 1954 to govern cases where the recipient, or server, of a notice has transferred their interest.

Information provided pursuant to a section 40 LTA 1954 request can plainly provide useful information for a landlord or tenant. In many cases, however, the parties will have sufficient information for the purposes of operating the Act or may have other available means for ascertaining the information. An eye should be kept to tactical considerations before serving a request for information: at the least, service of such a request may well prompt a recipient into taking legal advice. Sometimes, alerting the other side to one's intentions to serve a Section 25 Notice (or, as the case maybe, a Section 26 Request) in the future can be counter-productive by giving the counterparty the opportunity to consider its own position. (*e.g.* In some cases there maybe advantages for the other party in initiating the renewal/termination process by serving a Section 25 Notice or Section 26 Request, as applicable, first).

Requests under section 40 LTA 1954 need to be in the appropriate prescribed form. A person with an interest in reversion (whether immediately or not) on a tenancy of business premises is entitled to serve a notice on the tenant requiring the provision of the following information:

a) whether the tenant occupies the premises or any part of them wholly or partly for the purposes of a business carried on by him;

b) whether his tenancy has effect subject to any sub-tenancy on which his tenancy is immediately expectant and, if so –

(i) for what term it has effect (or, if it is terminable by notice, by what notice it can be terminated);

(ii) what is the rent payable under it;

(iii) who is the sub-tenant;

(iv) (to the best of his knowledge and belief) whether the sub-tenant is in occupation of the premises or part of the premises comprised in the sub-tenancy and, if not, what is the sub-tenant's address;

(v) whether an agreement is in force excluding in relation to the sub-tenancy the provisions of sections 24-28 LTA 1954;

(vi) whether a notice has been given under section 25 or 26(6) of LTA 1954, or a request made under section 26 in relation to the sub-tenancy and, if so, details of the notice or request; and

c) (to the best of his knowledge and belief) the name and address of any other person who owns an interest in reversion in any part of the premises.

Only certain classes of tenant are entitled to request information from reversioners: the tenants who are afforded rights under section 40(3) LTA 1954 are those who have a tenancy to which section 26(1) LTA 1954 applies (tenancies granted for a term certain exceeding a year or granted for a term certain and thereafter from year to year). Such tenants may serve on a reversioner, or reversioner's mortgagee in possession (if applicable) a notice requiring the provision of the following information from the reversioner:

a) whether he is the owner of the fee simple in respect of the premises or any part of them or the mortgagee in possession of such an owner;

b) if he is not, then (to the best of his knowledge and belief) –

(i) the name and address of the person who is or, as the case may be, his mortgagor's immediate landlord in respect of those premises or the part of which he or his mortgagor is not the owner in fee simple;

(ii) for what term his or his mortgagor's tenancy has effect and what is the earliest date (if any) at which that tenancy is terminable by notice to quit given by the landlord; and

(iii) whether a notice has been given under section 25 or 26 (6) of the LTA 1954, or request has been made under section 26 of the LTA 1954, in relation to the tenancy and, if so, details of the notice or request;

c) (to the best of his knowledge and belief) the name and address of any other person who owns an interest in reversion in any part of the premises; and

d) If he is a reversioner, whether there is a mortgagee in possession of his interest in the premises and, if so, (to the best of his knowledge and belief) what is the name and address of the mortgagee.

CHAPTER FIVE
SECURITY OF TENURE UNDER THE LTA 1954

In chapter 2 we discussed the tenancies to which Part II of the LTA 1954 applies by reference to section 23 of the Act. In this chapter, we consider how a tenant with a tenancy to which Part II applies enjoys security of tenure under the Act. We assume in this chapter that the relevant tenancy has not been excluded from the protection of sections 24-28 LTA 1954; as to which see Chapter 3.

The central provision by which security is conferred is section 24 (1) LTA 1954, which is worth setting out in full:

> *(1) A tenancy to which this Part of this Act applies shall not come to an end unless terminated in accordance with the provisions of this part of this Act; and, subject to the following provisions of this Act either the tenant of the landlord under such a tenancy may apply to the court for an order for the grant of a new tenancy –*
>
> > *(a) if the landlord has given notice under section 25 of this Act to terminate the tenancy, or*
> >
> > *(b) if the tenant has made a request for a new tenancy in accordance with section 26 of this Act.*

This section provides for a statutory continuation of the tenancy (i.e. the estate in land which the tenant holds at the date the tenancy continues under the Act). Because the estate in land itself is continued, the tenant's continuation tenancy can be assigned; whether such an assignment will be lawful will depend upon the provisions of the tenancy.

Section 24 LTA 1954 preserves certain methods of common law termination, namely:

- notice to quit given by the tenant;

- surrender (although note any *agreement* for surrender, as opposed to an actual surrender itself, will attract the attention of the contracting out regime in section 38A, as to which see chapter 3);

- forfeiture (including of a superior tenancy).

It is important to note the nine introductory words to section 24 LTA 1954: it is only a tenancy *to which Part II applie*s which shall not come to an end unless terminated in accordance with the provisions of the Act. To ascertain whether the tenancy *is* a tenancy to which Part II applies one goes back to the requirements in section 23 LTA 1954 (as to which, see Chapter 2). Providing those requirements are met as regards any part of the property comprised in the tenancy at the contractual term date, then the tenancy of the *whole* continues until terminated in accordance with the provisions of the Act. So if the tenant has (for example) sub-let part of the premises and is therefore not in occupation of the sub-let part but *is* in occupation for business purposes of the remainder at the contractual term date, then the tenancy of the whole (including the sub-let part) will continue under the LTA 1954.

In *Esselte AB and another v Pearl Assurance PLC* [1997] 1 WLR 891 the Court of Appeal held that it was crucial that Part II applied at the contractual term date: if the section 23 criteria were *not* met as at that date the tenancy was not one to which Part II applied and, therefore, the tenancy would *not* continue under the Act. In such a case the tenant has no more security of tenure than is afforded by the contractual term and has no right to remain in possession or to be granted a new tenancy under the Act.

This decision appears to be confirmed with the introduction, by the 2003 Order, of a new section 27(1A) which expressly provides that: '*Section 24 of this Act shall not have effect in relation to a tenancy for a term of years certain where the tenant is not in occupation of the property comprised in the tenancy at the time when, apart from this Act, the tenancy would come to an end by effluxion of time*' [Curiously, the section speaks of 'the property comprised in the tenancy", rather than '*any part of* the property comprised in the tenancy'. However, the tenant need only be in possession of a part of the premises for the tenancy of the whole to continue. *Woodfall's Landlord and Tenant* Volume II at 22.046 suggests that section 27(1A) LTA 1954 would be read as meaning any part of the property and it is respectfully suggested this is the correct view].

It can be particularly important, therefore, to ascertain whether the tenant is in occupation of any part of the premises comprised in the tenancy at the contractual term date.

If the landlord has the benefit of a contractual break clause then on proper exercise of the break the position is: (a) if the tenant *does not* satisfy the section 23 requirements at the break date then the tenancy will end; (b) if, however, the tenant *does* satisfy the section 23 requirements at that date then the tenancy will continue until terminated in accordance with the provisions of the Act. It has been held that a landlord can serve a composite notice in such a case seeking to exercise the break *and* give notice under Section 25 (see *Scholl MFG. Co. Ltd v Clifton (Slim-Line) Ltd* [1967] Ch 41). However, it is suggested that the cleaner practice is to serve two notices.

What if the section 23 requirements were met as at the contractual term date so that the tenancy continues by force of section 24 LTA 1954 but the tenant then goes out of occupation for business purposes in such a way that the section 23 requirements are no longer met? Does the tenancy automatically end? The answer is provided by section 24(3)(a): the tenancy does *not* automatically come to an end if it has been continued under the Act, but it can be terminated by not less than 3 and not more than 6 months' notice in writing given by the landlord to the tenant. The tenant cannot destabilise the efficacy of such a notice by (say) going back into occupation for business purposes because section 24(3)(b) LTA 1954 provides that where, at a time when Part II does not apply, the landlord gives a notice to quit the operation of the notice shall not be affected by reason of the tenancy becoming one to which the Act applies. (Indeed, section 24(3)(b) LTA 1954 applies more generally to pick up the situation where, for example, the LTA 1954 has never applied to a tenancy and the landlord serves a notice to quit).

To pursue an application for a new tenancy (whether following the service of a Section 25 notice or the making of a Section 26 Request) the tenant's tenancy must be one to which the Act continues to apply throughout the proceedings for the new tenancy: if the Act ceases to apply, the claim for a new tenancy is liable to be dismissed: see *I. & H. Caplan Ltd. v Caplan (No. 2)* [1963] 1 WLR 1247.

The question of whether a tenant has remained in occupation is plainly fact-sensitive and previously decided cases are of limited assistance (see *Grayism Holdings Ltd v P & O Property Holdings Ltd* [1996] AC 329, in which the House of Lords considered that the term 'occupied' had a connotation of physical use for business purposes but that this was 'not a test that will provide an answer in all cases'). In *I & H Caplan (No2)* Cross J gave examples of scenarios where premises may be *de facto* empty although still occupied for the purposes of the Act, namely: (1) where the tenant needed to vacate temporarily to allow repairs to be carried out; (2) where the tenant's business is seasonal (as to which, see *Teasedale v Walker* [1958] 1 WLR 1076) and the premises were closed in the winter. In *I & H Caplan No 2* itself (a protracted contested renewal) the tenant had in fact ceased trading from the premises but still had some stock on the premises; Cross J held on the particular facts of that case that the tenant remained in occupation. Given the critical importance for a tenant of the criteria being satisfied, it is suggested that the tenant (particularly during renewal proceedings when the landlord's antennae are likely to be engaged) would be best advised to maintain a clear physical business presence at the property. The greater the degree of physical presence, control and time devoted to the business activities being carried on, the stronger the tenant's position is likely to be in the event the landlord denies the tenant is in occupation.

CHAPTER SIX
FORFEITURE OF A TENANCY UNDER THE LTA 1954

Tenancies protected under the LTA 1954 can be terminated by forfeiture

Section 24(1) LTA 1954 provides that 'A tenancy to which this Part of this Act applies shall not come to an end unless terminated in accordance with the provisions of this Part of this Act'. This is then qualified by section 24(2):

> *(2) The last foregoing subsection shall not prevent the coming to an end of a tenancy by notice to quit given by the tenant, by surrender or forfeiture, or by the forfeiture of a superior tenancy unless—*
>
> > *(a) in the case of a notice to quit, the notice was given before the tenant had been in occupation in right of the tenancy for one month*

As is explored elsewhere, a landlord can experience difficulty terminating a tenancy protected by the LTA 1954. If it can forfeit the lease, it will often achieve a far more rapid outcome. Section 24(2) expressly retains the common law rules of forfeiture.

Forfeiture, however, is a technical part of the law. It is beyond the scope of this work to explore it in this chapter in any detail. Instead, this chapter will deal with the main issues that arise from the forfeiture of a tenancy protected by the LTA 1954.

Short outline of the law of forfeiture

If you are advising on a forfeiture case, it is worth reading a more specialist book on this area of the law as the general law is comprised of several particular rules. The Law Commission reported in this area in 1985 (Law Com. No. 142) and in 2006 (Cm 6946) but Parliament has not acted to legislate in respect of this complicated field for a considerable period of time, save in respect of residential tenancies.

The basis of the right

The law is based on a contractual right to 're-enter' a leasehold property. The landlord must reserve the right to 're-enter' the property, normally in the event of a tenant's breach of covenant. Re-entry brings the lease to an end, including any obligations to pay rent. It is possible for a landlord to re-enter the property either by physically going into the property (so called 'peaceable re-entry') or by serving a claim for re-entry on the tenant (re-entry by action). Peaceable re-entry of premises let as a dwelling is now unlawful: section 2 of the Protection from Eviction Act 1977. This restriction also applies to premises let for mixed residential and business uses: *Patel v Pirabakaran* [2006] 1 WLR 3112. Section 6 of the Criminal Law Act 1977 also prohibits the use of violence to re-enter premises where the person using the violence knows that there is someone present on the premises at the time who is opposed to the entry which the violence is intended to secure.

Normally the clause will allow for forfeiture for non-payment of rent or for breach of covenant. Some clauses provide for re-entry in the event of the tenant going into an insolvency event such as bankruptcy or liquidation. You should be aware, however, that depending on the form of insolvency there might be restrictions in relation to forfeiture as a consequence of the insolvency, depending on the type of insolvency involved.

Traditionally, forfeiture has been regarded as a draconian remedy, as it ends the leaseholder's interest in the land.

At common law, if a lease is forfeited any sub-tenancy under the lease is also destroyed. This makes the remedy particularly powerful if there are any unlawful sub-tenancies.

The landlord must unequivocally elect to bring the lease to an end to exercise the right of re-entry. It is open to the landlord to elect to allow the lease to continue (for example, if it will be difficult to find a new tenant or where rents are falling), and to simply bring a claim in respect of the breach of covenant.

Waiver

Once a ground for forfeiture has arisen and the landlord is aware of this, he or she must be careful not to 'waive' the right to forfeit the lease. Waiver is a technical area of the law. In summary, a landlord must be careful not to do anything that affirms the ongoing existence of the lease. The classic example of waiver is acceptance of, or a demand for, rent: *Central Estates (Belgravia) Ltd v Woolgar (No 2)* [1972] 1 WLR 1048. Even if rent is accepted on a 'without prejudice' basis, it can still effect a waiver: *Segal Securities Ltd v Thoseby* [1963] 1 QB 887. Only a lessor can exercise the remedy of the commercial rent arrears recovery ("CRAR") procedure under section 72 of the Tribunals, Courts and Enforcement Act 2007 (which replaced common law distress) and cannot be exercised after termination of the lease by forfeiture. In principle, it amounts to an unequivocal affirmation of the continuation of the lease, just as the levying of distress at common law had done: *Thirunavukkrasu v Brar* [2019] EWCA Civ 2032, [2020] Ch 56.

When acceptance of rent constituted waiver was considered in *Faiz v Burnley Borough Council* [2021] EWCA Civ 55; [2021] 2 WLR 1115. The lease contained an absolute prohibition on sub-letting. Rent arrears for the 1 October quarter day accrued. On 18 October, the landlord became aware that a sub-tenancy had been unlawfully granted. The landlord served a section 146 notice, relying on the grant of the sub-lease, but then made a demand for insurance rent encompassing only the period ending on 18 October. It was held, at first instance and in the Court of Appeal, that the landlord had not waived the forfeiture. It was held (at [37] by Lewison LJ) that that waiver takes place where the landlord demands or accepts rent which accrued due after the date of a breach known to the landlord. Where the breach consists of an unlawful sub-letting, the landlord must know not only that the sub-letting has taken place, but also that the rent demanded or accepted accrued due after the date of the breach, to establish waiver. The burden of proof in establishing waiver lies on the tenants: in that case, they did not establish that the sub-letting had occurred before the insurance rent became due.

Waiver of the right to forfeit is not the same as waiver of the breach and a landlord can still bring a claim for damages. It does, however, prevent the landlord from re-entering the premises.

Waiver of a continuing breach (such as a breach of a repair covenant) does not prevent the right to forfeit from arising from day to day. On the other hand, 'once and for all' breaches, once waived, cannot be relied upon by the landlord in respect of re-entry.

A landlord can only waive a right to forfeit in respect of a breach that it knows about. A landlord will probably be deemed to have the knowledge of its agent for the purpose of forfeiture. Waiver is judged objectively: the intention of the landlord is irrelevant.

Section 146 Law of Property Act 1925

For commercial tenancies, the most important statutory restriction on the landlord's ability to forfeit a lease is section 146 of the Law of Property Act 1925.

Section 146 LPA 1925 does not apply to the following cases:

- re-entry for the non-payment of rent (s146(11));
- re-entry where the condition for forfeiture is the bankruptcy of the lessee (s146(9));
- leases for agricultural or pastoral land (s146(9)(a));
- leases for mines or minerals (s146(9)(b));
- leases for houses used or intended to be used as public-houses or beershops (s146(9)(c));
- a lease of a house let as a dwelling-house, with the use of any furniture, books, works of art, or other chattels not being in the nature of fixtures (s146(9)(d));

- a lease of any property with respect to which the personal qualifications of the tenant are of importance for the preservation of the value or character of the property, or on the ground of neighbourhood to the lessor, or to any person holding under him (s146(9)(e)).

Where section 146 applies, a right of re-entry or forfeiture under a clause in the lease for breach of covenant is not enforceable unless the landlord serves on the tenant a notice:

a) specifying the breach complained of; and

b) if the breach is capable of remedy, requiring the lessee to remedy the breach; and

c) in any case, requiring the tenant to pay monetary compensation for the breach;

and the tenants fails to remedy the breach within a reasonable period of time afterwards (if the breach is capable of being remedied) and fails to make financial compensation for the breach. (section 146(1)).

It is therefore important for the landlord to consider, when drafting a section 146 notice:

- whether the breach is one that is capable of remedy: here, there is a considerable body of case law about different kinds of breaches;

- how long a 'reasonable period' will be;

- what financial compensation is being sought.

In respect of forfeiture for disrepair, section 18(2) of the Landlord and Tenant Act 1927 provides that a right of re-entry or forfeiture shall not be enforceable unless the landlord proves that the fact that a section 146 notice had been served on the lessee was known either:

a) to the lessee; or

b) to an under-lessee holding under an under-lease which reserved a nominal reversion only to the lessee; or

c) to the person who last paid the rent due under the lease either on his own behalf or as agent for the lessee or under-lessee;

and that a time reasonably sufficient to enable the repairs to be executed had elapsed since the time when the fact of the service of the notice came to the knowledge of any such person. For the purpose of this provision, where a notice has been sent by registered post addressed to a person at his last known place of abode in the United Kingdom, then, for the purposes of this subsection, that person is deemed to have had knowledge of the fact that the notice had been served as from the time at which the letter would have been delivered in the ordinary course of post unless the contrary is proved.

Further, where a landlord seeks forfeiture in respect of a breach of a repair covenant where the lease was granted for a term of more than seven years and three or more years remain unexpired, the tenant may serve a counter-notice to a section 146 notice under section 1(2) of the Leasehold Property (Repairs) Act 1938 claiming the benefit of that Act. Once the counter-notice is served, the landlord then can only exercise a right of re-entry with the leave of the court: section 1(3) of the LP(R)A 1938. Further, that section 146 notice must contain wording to the effect that the lessee is entitled under the LP(R)A 1938 to serve on the lessor a counter-notice claiming the benefit of this Act, and a statement in the like characters specifying the time within which, and the manner in which, under the LP(R)A 1938 a counter-notice may be served and specifying the name and address for service of the lessor. This wording must be written in characters not less conspicuous than those used in any other part of the notice. (although section 1 LP(R)A 1938 originally only applied to small houses, its effect was extended to all leases by section 51 LTA 1954).

If the tenant fails to comply with a valid section 146 notice, the landlord is free to forfeit the lease, either by peaceable re-entry or by commencing and serving an action.

Non-payment of rent

No section 146 notice is required. At common law the landlord cannot enforce a right of re-entry for breach of covenant to pay rent until he or she has made a formal demand for the rent. This must be performed at the demised premises or at the place specified in the lease for the payment of rent and must require the exact sum due to be paid before sunset on the last due date for due payment (unless more than half a year's rent is in arrears, the power under section 72(1) of the Tribunals, Courts and Enforcement Act 2007 (commercial rent arrears recovery) is available but there are not sufficient goods on the premises to recover the arrears by that power: section 210 of the Common Law Procedure Act 1852 for proceedings in the High Court; section 139(1) of the County Courts Act 1984). Most modern re-entry clauses get around this problem by confirming that the right to re-enter arises whether the rent has been formally demanded or not.

Relief from forfeiture

If a landlord has validly forfeited a lease, the onus is on the tenant to apply for relief from forfeiture. Relief from forfeiture retrospectively restores a tenancy that has been forfeited. The period during which it is not known whether a forfeiture is going to be effective, for example, if the allegations of breach of covenant are denied, or relief against forfeiture may be granted is often referred to as the 'twilight period': Associated Deliveries Ltd v Harrison (1985) 50 P. & C.R. 91.

Section 146(2) LPA 1925 provides:

> *(2) Where a lessor is proceeding, by action or otherwise, to enforce such a right of re-entry or forfeiture, the lessee may, in the lessor's action, if any, or in any action brought by himself, apply to the court for relief; and the court may grant or refuse relief, as the court, having regard to the proceedings and conduct of the parties under the foregoing provisions of this section, and to all the other circumstances, thinks fit; and in case of relief may grant it on such terms, if any, as to costs, expenses, damages, compensation, penalty, or otherwise, including the granting of an injunction to restrain any like breach in the future, as the court, in the circumstances of each case, thinks fit.*

The application for relief from forfeiture can be made as a free-standing claim or as a counterclaim to a landlord's claim for forfeiture by action. The application can be made from the moment a section 146 notice is served: *Packwood Transport Ltd v Beauchamp Place Limited* (1978) 36 P & CR 112.

Relief from forfeiture is discretionary and the conduct of the lessee is relevant. It was made clear in *Hyman v Rose* [1912] AC 623 by Lord Loreburn that the discretion is wide and is not to be subjected to rigid rules. This was re-confirmed by the Court of Appeal in *Magnic Ltd v Ul-Hassan and Malik* [2015] EWCA Civ 224. See also *Shiloh Spinners Ltd v Harding* [1973] AC 691, where Lord Wilberforce summarised the factors that a court will take into account when considering whether to grant relief.

A sub-tenant is also able to apply under section 146(4) LPA 1925. A sub-tenant might be able to obtain a vesting order creating a new tenancy making the sub-tenant the tenant of the landlord. Mortgagees are also able to apply for relief.

If the tenant seeks relief from forfeiture for non-payment of rent, he or she will be able to seek relief under section 138 of the County Courts Act 1984 for cases where the lessor is proceeding by action in the county court to enforce against a lessee a right of re-entry in the county court:

- if the lessee pays into court or to the lessor not less than five clear days before the return day of a hearing for a claim for forfeiture all the rent in arrear and the costs of the action, the action shall cease, and the lessee shall hold the land according to the existing lease: section 138(2) CCA 1984. This relief is automatic;

- otherwise, if this deadline is missed or if the landlord has peaceably re-entered the tenancy, the court can order possession of the land to be given to the lessor at the expiration of such period, not being less than four weeks from the date of the order, as the court thinks fit, unless within that period the lessee pays into court or to the lessor all the rent in arrear and the costs of the action: section 138(3) CCA 1984. This period can be extended: section 138(4)

CCA 1984. Subject to the period being fixed by the court, this relief is automatic;

- it is possible to obtain relief even after the landlord has recovered possession on application to the court: section 138(9A) CCA 1984. This relief is at the discretion of the court. There is a 6-month time limit for such an application.

A sub-tenant is also entitled to apply under section 138 CCA 1984: section 140 CCA 1984. Where the landlord has enforced against the lessee by re-entry without action (i.e. peaceable re-entry) for non-payment of rent, the lessee may apply to the county court for relief at any time within 6 months from the date on which the lessor re-entered. On any such application the court may, if it thinks fit, grant to the lessee such relief as the High Court could have granted.

If the matter is, exceptionally, proceeding in the High Court, you should have regard to the like provisions in section 38 of the Senior Courts Act 1981 (where the landlord is proceeding in the High Court) and sections 210 and 212 of the Common Law Procedure Act 1852 (which are concerned with cases where the landlord has proceeded, or is proceeding, in court, and have no application to cases of peaceable re-entry, and which are also expressly limited to cases where at least one half year's rent is in arrear). There is no statutory provision available to the High Court in cases of peaceable re-entry, and in such a case it retains, and exercises, its equitable jurisdiction. Accordingly, in *Pineport Ltd v Grangeglen Ltd* [2016] L&TR 28 relief in the High Court was granted despite a 14 month delay.

These provisions were reviewed by the Court of Appeal in *Keshwala v Bhalsod* [2021] EWCA Civ 492. It was noted (at [42]) that section 138 CCA 1984 does not apply where the landlord has recovered possession without first obtaining a court order. Where the landlord has peaceably re-entered, the relevant provision is section 139(2) of the County Courts Act 1984 which enables the lessee to apply to the County Court for relief within 6 months from possession being taken. It was confirmed in that case that simply because a tenant has applied within the 6 month time limit does not mean that the tenant will be taken to have acted reasonably promptly. It was held (at [59]) that "*Compliance with the six month time limit on applications for relief is a necessary, but not a sufficient, precondition for relief. It is incumbent on any applicant for relief, whether a lessee or a person deriving title from a lessee, to make application with all due diligence and keep the lessor informed of his intentions... and, if there is any apparent delay, in his evidence fully to explain it.*" In that case, the tenants had applied within six months of the landlord recovering possession by peaceable re-entry on the ground of rent arrears. The Court of Appeal confirmed that the first instance judge was correct to refuse relief from forfeiture as the tenants had not established that they had applied reasonably promptly and *Pineport* was distinguished as being a situation where the landlord had forfeited and then done nothing with the property – just "stood by to await events"

Particular features of the law of forfeiture where a tenancy protected by the LTA 1954 is involved

If a landlord forfeits a head tenancy this may also bring a sub-tenancy to an end, even if the sub-tenancy is protected by the LTA 1954. This was confirmed in *Hill v Griffin* [1987] 1 EGLR 81, CA.

Where the landlord seeks to forfeit the tenancy, both the tenant and the subtenant have the right to apply for relief from forfeiture under section 146 of the Law of Property Act 1925. A subtenant protected by the LTA 1954 can still seek relief. Section 146(4) prevents the grant of a lease for any longer term than a sub-tenant had under their original sub-lease. Frequently, however, the subtenant's original term will have expired and it will be occupying as a statutory continuation tenant. For the purpose of section 146(4), the 'term' of the original sub-lease includes the extension imposed by the LTA 1954: *Cadogan v Dimovic* [1984] 1 WLR 609. The court has jurisdiction under section 146(4) of the Act of 1925 to make a vesting order for a new term of appropriate duration but within the limits of the extension imposed by the LTA 1954.

This period might very well be short. As was noted in *Hill v Griffin*, if the term of the head tenancy has come to an end due to forfeiture and the subtenancy is a statutory continuation tenancy, all that the subtenant can seek is the term which the subtenant would have had but for the forfeiture: in the case of a business tenancy this term is, by virtue of section 24(1), the period which would elapse before the tenancy could be terminated in accordance with the LTA 1954 following the expiry of the term granted by the under-lease. In *Hill v Griffin* this was a period of one month.

If the landlord has brought a claim for forfeiture, then as long as the claim for forfeiture and any counterclaim for relief has not been finally disposed of, the tenant is entitled to apply to the court for the grant of a new tenancy: *Meadows v Clerical Medical and General Life Assurance Society* [1981] Ch. 70. In *Baglarbasi v Deedmethod* [1991] 2 EGLR 71, it was held that a landlord was entitled to serve a section 25 notice after commencing forfeiture proceedings by action: it was held that the landlord is not entitled to do anything which is inconsistent with his intention to put an end to the lease. If, however, another ground for determining it becomes available he can rely on it, for that is not inconsistent with his intention.

CHAPTER SEVEN

OTHER METHODS OF TERMINATION: DISCLAIMER, MERGER AND FRUSTRATION

Section 24(1) LTA 1954 provides that 'A tenancy to which this Part of this Act applies shall not come to an end unless terminated in accordance with the provisions of this Part of this Act' and, although section 24(2) preserves 'notice to quit given by the tenant, by surrender or forfeiture, or by the forfeiture of a superior tenancy', some more obscure methods by which a common law commercial tenancy can be terminated are not mentioned. Although these are unlikely to be encountered in practice, they are mentioned here to provide a starting point for any research into these areas of landlord and tenant law.

Disclaimer

Where a trustee in bankruptcy or a liquidator in both compulsory and voluntary liquidation takes on property that is 'onerous', the insolvency practitioner can 'disclaim' the property even though he or she has taken possession of it, tried to sell it, or otherwise exercised rights of ownership: section 178 of the Insolvency Act 1986 for liquidation, section 315 IA 1986 for bankruptcy.

Disclaimer determines, from the date of the disclaimer, the rights, interests and liabilities of the company or the debtor in the property disclaimed. It does not affect the rights or liabilities of any other person, except so far as is necessary for the purpose of releasing the company from any liability.

Any person sustaining loss or damage in consequence of the operation of a disclaimer is deemed a creditor in the insolvency to the extent of the loss or damage and accordingly may prove for the loss or damage.

Disclaimer operates by way of notice by the insolvency practitioner.

Restriction on disclaimer

The insolvency practitioner can be barred from disclaiming the property if a person interested in the property has applied in writing to the insolvency practitioner or one of his predecessors requiring the insolvency practitioner or that predecessor to decide whether he will disclaim or not, and the period of 28 days beginning with the day on which that application was made, or such longer period as the court may allow, has expired without a notice of disclaimer having been given under this section in respect of that property.

Onerous property

'Onerous property' includes:

- any unprofitable contract;

- any other property of the company which is:
    - unsaleable;
    - not readily saleable;
    - such that it may give rise to a liability to pay money or perform any other onerous act.

'Property' includes leasehold property as well as freehold property. In *Hunt v Conwy County Borough Council* [2014] 1 WLR 254 the liquidator validly disclaimed a seaside pier which, as freehold property, escheated to the Crown. If repair notices had been served on the pier, which was in a perilous state of repair, it was likely that the condition of the pier was such as to give rise to a liability to pay money or perform any other onerous act, making it onerous property.

Third parties affected by a disclaimer

There are a number classes of persons who might be affected by a disclaimer. They potentially include:

- Tenants and subtenants of the insolvent party;

- Guarantors / sureties of the insolvent party;
- The landlord of the insolvent party;
- The mortgagee of the disclaimed property.

In *Hindcastle Ltd v Barbara Attenborough Associates Ltd and others* [1997] AC 70, the owner of a leasehold property went into creditors' voluntary liquidation and the lease was disclaimed. The landlord brought proceedings against the original tenant who had been demised the property, its successor who conveyed the lease to the insolvent company, and the surety of the successor / assignor for arrears of rent arising before and after the disclaimer. The House of Lords held that when the lease was disclaimed it determined and the reversion accelerated, but the rights and liabilities of others (such as guarantors and original tenants) remained as though the lease had continued and not been determined. If no vesting order is made and the landlord takes possession, the liabilities of other persons to pay the rent and perform the tenant's covenants will come to an end so far as the future is concerned. If the landlord acts in this way, he is no longer the 'involuntary recipient' of a disclaimed lease, but has now demonstrated that he regards the lease as ended for all purposes.

Subtenants

It was also held in *Hindcastle* that the subtenant's interest continued, unaffected by the determination of the tenant's interest. The subtenant's right to remain in possession of the disclaimed property is not, however, a continuation of the sublease (*Re AE Realisations* [1987] 3 All ER 83. It only remains in existence so far as is necessary to support the subtenant's right to remain in occupation. The subtenant's rights and obligations to the insolvent tenant (its immediate landlord) are extinguished, but his or her right to remain in possession is dependent upon complying with the covenants in the headlease, including paying of rent, even if that rent is greater than the sublease rent. If the subtenant does not comply, the landlord will be able to enforce the terms of the disclaimed lease against the subtenant.

If the subtenancy is protected by the LTA 1954, it can only be determined by one of the methods included in the 1954 Act, which does not include disclaimer of the headlease. Furthermore, as the superior landlord does not immediately become the immediate landlord of the subtenant, so that it is arguable that it only becomes the competent tenant when the remaining term of the headlease reaches 14 months or less. If this is right, it would place the superior landlord in a difficult position. Both the superior landlord and the subtenant may wish to consider whether it is appropriate to apply for a vesting order.

Vesting orders

The IA 1986 allows for a person who claims an interest in the disclaimed property or any person who is under any liability in respect of the disclaimed property, not being a liability discharged by the disclaimer, to apply for an order for the vesting of the disclaimed property in a person entitled to it or a trustee for such a person, or a person subject to such a liability. Such an application must be made within three months of the applicant becoming aware of the disclaimer or of his receiving notice of it, whichever is the earlier: see Insolvency Rules 2016, rule 19.11.

Merger

Whereas a surrender occurs where the landlord acquires the lease, merger occurs where the tenant acquires the reversion, or a third party acquires both the lease and the reversion. The effect of merger is that the lease is absorbed and destroyed by the reversion. It is noteworthy that in equity merger is a matter of intention: there is a presumption against merger if it is against that person's interest.

The case of *EDF Energy Networks (EPN) Plc v BOH Ltd* [2011] L & TR 15 is discussed below in the context of section 25 Notices. EDF had become the tenant of three plots of land and had a right of way over a fourth. The freehold titles to the four plots were sold to separate buyers and the reversions became severed. EDF purchased the freehold to one plot; the other three plots were purchased by BOH and LC. EDF's contractual term expired and the lease continued under section 24 LTA 1954. It was held that BOH and LC could not serve a section 25 Notice without EDF being a party. In the absence of intention, the presumption against merger if it is against that person's interest applied: EDF's leasehold interest therefore did not merge with its freehold interest.

Frustration

In *National Carriers Ltd v Panalpina (Northern) Ltd* [1981] AC 675 the House of Lords held that, in principle, a commercial lease could be determined by frustration, although this would only apply in rare circumstances. In *Cricklewood Property and Investment Trust Ltd v. Leighton's Investment Trust Ltd* [1945] AC 221, at 229 Viscount Simon L.C., who favoured the extension of the doctrine of frustration to leaseholds, nevertheless considered it likely to be limited to cases where 'some vast convulsion of nature swallowed up the property altogether, or buried it in the depths of the sea.' As a consequence, it is very unlikely to be encountered in practice, especially in the context of LTA 1954 leases, and the interaction with the statutory regime is unclear.

In *Canary Wharf (BP4) T1 Ltd v European Medicines Agency* [2019] EWHC 335 (Ch); [2019] L & TR 14 the tenant ("EMA") contended that by reason of the withdrawal of the United Kingdom from the European Union, when Brexit occurred, the lease of its premises in Canary Wharf and the necessary relocation of the EMA away from the UK amounted to a frustration of its lease. Marcus Smith J held that there were no constraints on EMA's capacity or *vires* such as to cause the lease to be frustrated; even if those constraints on capacity existed, they were irrelevant to the question of frustration by reason of supervening illegality; but if he had been wrong on these points, the legal effects on the EMA of the UK's withdrawal from the European Union could have been, but were not, ameliorated by the European Union and this failure to do so was relevant to the question of frustration and rendered the frustration of the lease self-induced.

Section 24 LTA 1954 states that 'A tenancy to which this Part of this Act applies shall not come to an end unless terminated in accordance with the provisions of this Part of this Act': it does not refer to frustration. If the frustrating event brings to an end the tenant's occupation (and it is difficult to see how frustration would apply if it did not), however, it will cease to be a tenancy to which the LTA 1954 applies. On one interpretation, the contractual term will be ended by the frustrating event, so that the tenant will still have to consider which parts of section 27 would apply to his or her situation to bring the statutory continuation tenancy to an end.

CHAPTER EIGHT

TENANT'S APPLICATION FOR A NEW TENANCY

Without more, a LTA 1954 tenancy will simply continue on the same terms past its contractual term date. There will be occasions when either the landlord or the tenant wants a new lease to be granted. For example, the tenant may want a new, longer term in order to obtain greater security. The LTA 1954 allows a tenant to apply for a new tenancy.

Section 26 request for a new tenancy

The tenant can request a new tenancy under section 26 LTA 1954. It is not possible to make this request under section 26 if a section 25 Notice has already been served: instead, the tenant must apply to the court. Likewise, it is not possible to serve a section 26 notice if the tenant has already given notice to quit or notice under section 27.

At the same time, once a tenant has made a valid section 26 request, it is not possible for the landlord to serve a section 25 notice or for the tenant to serve a notice to quit or a notice under section 27: section 26(4).

The effect of a section 26 Notice is to terminate the tenancy immediately before the date specified in the request for the beginning of the new tenancy. It then continues in the interim under section 64.

Eligibility criteria

The tenant must satisfy the following criteria before serving a section 26 Notice:

- The tenancy granted must be:
    - for a term of years certain, exceeding one year (whether or not continued by section 24); OR

  - for a term of years certain, and thereafter from year to year (section 26(1)).

A holder of a fixed term of less than six months will be excluded from the LTA 1954 by section 43(3) in any case.

Start date of the new tenancy

- The tenant's request for a new tenancy shall be for a tenancy that starts on a date (a) not more than 12 months, and (b) not less than 6 months, after the making of the request.

- The start date must not be earlier than the date on which the contractual term will come to an end, or could be brought to an end by a tenant's notice to quit (section 26(2)).

The reason for this is that section 26 brings the current tenancy to an end: this can only be done if the current tenancy can be ended i.e. the contractual term will have finished by the start of the new tenancy. The 6–12 month rule echoes the same provision in section 25.

The contents of the request

The new tenancy will start at least 6 months from when the request is made, but not more than 12 months. The date itself is specified in the tenant's notice.

- The date on which the new tenancy will start must not be earlier than the date on which the current tenancy would come to an end by effluxion of time, or could be brought to an end by a tenant's notice to quit (section 26(2)).

- It is not possible to specify a start date that falls before the end of the current contractual term, or when a tenant could terminate the tenancy with its own notice to quit.

  This provision was explored in *Garston v Scottish Widows Fund & Life Assurance Society* [1998] 1 WLR 1583. The lease was for a term of 20 years with a tenant's break clause at 10 years. The Court of Appeal held that the tenant had validly activated the break clause, ending the contractual term. It then went on to hold that the second limb (tenant's notice to quit) referred to notices ending periodic tenancies and not break clauses.

In *Fast Drinks Ltd v Cetyl International Group Inc* [2016] EWHC 3501 (QB), the term of the headlease expired on 16 January 2016 but was subject to a break clause. The lease term in question expired on 15 January 2016. The break clause was activated, bringing the headlease to an end: the lease itself was continued by section 24(1) LTA 1954. The tenant's Section 26 Notice named 1 July 2015 as the date for the commencement of the new tenancy. The notice was held to be valid even though this was before 16 January 2016. The proviso in section 26(2) that the start date for the claimed new tenancy must not be earlier than the effluxion date of the current tenancy was held not to apply, as apart from the LTA 1954, the tenancy would not come to an end by effluxion of time.

- The tenant's request must be served on the competent landlord.

- The tenant's request must be made in the prescribed form (currently Form 3 of the Landlord and Tenant Act 1954, Part 2 (Notices) Regulations 2004).

- The notice must set out the tenant's proposals as to:
    - The property to be comprised in the new tenancy (either the whole or part of the property comprised in the current tenancy).
    - The rent payable under the new tenancy.
    - The terms of the new tenancy.

      The notice does not have to specify the whole of the premises: a tenant can renew only part of the property.

- The notice must specify the date for the commencement of the new tenancy.

- Once a tenant has served a section 26 Notice it cannot withdraw it and serve a second request: *Polyviou v Seeley* [1980] 1 WLR 55. This case explains that is because once a valid request had been served, section 26(5) operates to determine the current tenancy immediately before the date specified for commencement of the new tenancy unless the tenant applied to the court for a new tenancy.

Landlord's response

Within 2 months of the tenant making its request for a new tenancy, the landlord may give notice to the tenant that he will oppose an application to the court for the grant of a new tenancy. The landlord has to specify in its notice which of the section 30 grounds it will rely on to oppose the application.

There is no prescribed form for the landlord's notice. It cannot subsequently be amended or withdrawn and will bind anyone who subsequently takes on the landlord's interest.

If a landlord fails to serve a notice in opposition it will lose the right to oppose the application for a new tenant. The landlord will still be able to argue about the terms of the new tenancy.

CHECKLIST: Section 26 Notice

- A tenant cannot make a request for a new tenancy under section 26 if a landlord has given notice under section 25. Instead, the tenant must apply to the court for a new tenancy.

- The tenancy itself must satisfy the eligibility criteria under section 26(1).

- The date when the new tenancy starts must be specified by the tenant as being at least 6 months, but not more than 12 months, after the making of the request.

- The specified date must not be earlier than when the tenancy would end by effluxion of time or could be brought to an end by notice to quit given by the tenant.

- The tenant's request for a new tenancy must be made on the correct form.

- The form must contain the tenant's proposals as to the terms of the new tenancy, including the rent.

- The landlord must respond within two months of the tenant's notice by giving notice to the tenant whether it will oppose the grant of a new tenancy.

- If the landlord is opposing the grant of a new tenancy, the landlord's notice must state which of the section 30 grounds the landlord will rely upon.

Tenant's application to the court for a new tenancy

Following:

a) a section 25 Notice opposing the grant of a new tenancy to the tenant;

b) a section 26 Notice requesting a new tenancy;

the tenant must apply to the court if it wants a new tenancy. If the tenant does not apply within the prescribed time limits the tenancy will come to an end (section 25(1); section 26(5)). **It is very important not to overlook this, especially where the tenant has made the request for a new tenancy.** The strict time limits applicable to an application are discussed below.

The application is made under section 24(1):

24 Continuation of tenancies to which Part II applies and grant of new tenancies

(1) A tenancy to which this Part of this Act applies shall not come to an end unless terminated in accordance with the provisions of this Part of this Act; and, subject to the following provisions of this Act either the tenant or the landlord under such a tenancy may apply to the court for an order for the grant of a new tenancy—

(a) if the landlord has given notice under section 25 of this Act to terminate the tenancy, or

(b) if the tenant has made a request for a new tenancy in accordance with section twenty-six of this Act.

Neither the landlord nor the tenant may make an application to the court under section 24(1) if the other has made such an application and the application has been served: section 24(2A). Likewise, neither the tenant nor the landlord may make such an application if the landlord has made an application under section 29(2) and the application has been served: section 24(2B). This prevents the court having to deal with multiple applications about the same tenancy.

The landlord may not withdraw an application under subsection (1) above unless the tenant consents to its withdrawal: section 24(2C).

Time limits

The provisions for applications to court are contained in section 29 and 29B. Section 29(1) states that if the court does grant a new tenancy, it shall make an order for the grant of a new tenancy and for the termination of the current tenancy immediately before the commencement of the new tenancy.

Time limits following a section 25 Notice

Following a section 25 Notice, a tenant must apply to the court for a new tenancy under section 24(1) before the date specified in the notice. If the tenant does not, a new tenancy will either be imposed on the terms given in the landlord's section 25 Notice where it does not oppose a new tenancy, or the tenancy will be terminated if the landlord does oppose a new tenancy.

Especially where the landlord opposes the grant of a new tenancy, you would be well advised to diarise and timetable the date given in the section 25 Notice.

Time limits following a section 26 Notice

Section 29A(1) states that that the court shall not entertain an application by the tenant under section 24(1) if it is made after the end of the 'statutory period', that is, where the tenant made a request for a new tenancy under section 26 of this Act, immediately before the date specified in his request.

A tenant cannot, however, make an application within two months of making its request for a new tenancy under section 26, unless the application is made after the landlord has given a notice under section 26(6). The purpose of this provision is to give the landlord time to respond to the section 26 request.

Agreed extensions

After the landlord has given a Section 25 Notice or the tenant has made a section 26 request but before the date specified in the notice has ended, the parties may agree to extend the time for an application to the court: section 29B(1). This agreement must be reached before the time limit expires. The time limit can be further extended by agreement (section 29B(2)) but this agreement must be made before the end of the already agreed time limit.

CHECKLIST: time periods

- Following a section 25 Notice, the tenant has until the date given in the notice to apply to the court for a new tenancy.

- Following a section 26 Notice, the tenant must apply for a new tenancy from the court before the date specified in the section 26 Notice. If it does not, the tenancy will simply expire: section 26(5).

- A tenant cannot make an application within two months of making its request for a new tenancy under section 26, unless the application is made after the landlord has given a notice under section 26(6).

- The time limit for an application to the court can be extended by agreement (section 29B) but you must be careful to either apply or further extend the deadline within the new time limit: you cannot retrospectively agree to extend the time limit for the court application.

CHAPTER NINE
TENANT'S TERMINATION OF A TENANCY

As noted elsewhere, a tenancy protected by the LTA 1954 does not come to an end by effluxion of time but can only be terminated by one of the methods prescribed by the Act. As a consequence, the LTA 1954 contains a code governing the situation where a tenant simply wishes to leave the demised property at the end of the term, or wishes to exercise a break notice.

Notice that a tenant does not wish a tenancy to be continued

A tenant can give a written notice no later than three months before the end of the contractual term of a fixed term tenancy that he or she does not wish the tenancy to continue. This has the effect of disapplying section 24 LTA 1954 so that the tenancy comes to an end by way of effluxion of time as in the normal way (section 27(1) LTA 1954). It is not possible to give such a notice before a tenant has been in occupation for a month.

Tenant moving out of the property by the end of the contractual term

If the tenant is not in occupation of the property comprised in the tenancy at the time when the contractual term comes to an end, section 24 is disapplied so that there is no statutory continuation: section 27(1A).

A tenant should be careful, however, to ensure that he or she leaves the property in vacant possession so that there is no 'occupation' of the property, otherwise section 24 might be engaged to extend the tenancy, and hence liability for rent and other obligations under the tenancy.

In *Single Horse Properties Ltd v Surrey County Council* [2002] 2 EGLR 43, the Court of Appeal explored the interaction between section 27 and section 25. The contractual term was due to expire on 24 June 2000. The landlord served a section 25 Notice also expiring on 24 June 2000. The tenant served, in accordance with the LTA 1954 at the time, a counternotice and applied to the court for a new tenancy. However, on 13 June 2000, the tenant vacated the building and on 16 June 2000 its agent returned the keys. The issue was whether the tenant was liable for a further three months' rent from the dismissal of its application for a new tenancy under section 64, or whether the tenancy determined on 24 June 2000. The Court of Appeal held that a section 25 Notice is of no effect if the tenancy is not continued by section 24(1); as the lease had determined on 24 June 2000, there was no interim continuation. Arden LJ did warn, however, that:

> *A tenant who has served a counternotice under section 25, and made an application to the court, should inform the landlord if he ceases to occupy the demised premises before the term date so that the application to the court can be dismissed. If a tenant fails to do this, and the landlord is led by the tenant's conduct to believe that the tenant continues in occupation, there is a risk that, in the events that happened, as in Benedictus v Jalaram Ltd (1989) 58 P&CR 330, the tenant will be held to have estopped himself from denying that he was in occupation at the term date, and be liable for continuing rent accordingly.*

Terminating a statutory continuation tenancy

A tenancy which was granted for a term of years certain which is being continued by section 24 LTA 1954 does not come to an end simply because the tenant ends his or her occupation: section 27(2) LTA 1954. Instead, the tenant must give not less than three months' notice in writing to his or her immediate landlord.

This notice can be given before or after the date of the termination of the contractual term. It cannot, however, be given by a tenant who has been in occupation for less than a month.

Section 27(3) LTA 1954 deals with apportionment of rent when a notice is given under this provision. Any rent payable in respect of a period which begins before, and ends after, the tenancy is terminated shall be apportioned, and any rent paid by the tenant in excess of the amount apportioned to the period before termination shall be recoverable by him or her.

Service of a section 26 notice

Although not an appropriate use of the section 26 Notice procedure, it is worth recalling that if a section 26 Notice is served, the tenancy ends on the date given in the notice unless a court application is made.

Discontinuance

If a tenant applies to the court for a new tenancy and then discontinues the application, the tenancy will come to an end three months later and no section 27 notice is required: see chapter 20.

If the landlord applies to court for the grant of a new tenancy and the new tenant does not want one, the tenant must inform the court that he does not want a new tenancy: section 29(5) LTA 1954. This takes effect as a discontinuance by the tenant, which can have costs consequences if steps have been taken in the litigation: in *Lay v Drexler* [2007] 2 EGLR 46, discussed in chapter 20.

CHAPTER TEN
LANDLORD'S NOTICE TO TERMINATE A TENANCY

Section 25 notice

For a landlord to terminate a tenancy protected by Part II of the LTA 1954, it is necessary to serve a notice under section 25 LTA 1954. If such a notice is not served and the tenant does not serve his or her own notice terminating the tenancy or leaves the protection of the Act, even a tenancy that would expire due to effluxion of time would be continued by section 24 LTA 1954. Many disputes arising under the LTA 1954, therefore, start with a section 25 Notice.

Must use a prescribed form

Section 25 Notices must be in the prescribed form or in a form 'substantially to the like effect'. These are prescribed by the Landlord and Tenant Act 1954, Part 2 (Notices) Regulations 2004 (SI 2004/1005) (see section 66(1) LTA 1954). The forms are found in Schedule 2, with their purposes set out in Schedule 1. The forms include explanatory notes which must be included on the notice: section 66(2) LTA 1954.

Form 1 is used to end a tenancy under section 25, where the landlord is not opposed to the grant of a new tenancy.

Form 2 is used to end a tenancy under section 25, where the landlord is opposed to the grant of a new tenancy and the tenant is not entitled under the Leasehold Reform Act 1967 to buy the freehold or an extended lease.

It is very important to read the notes that accompany the forms and to fill in the notices as accurately as possible.

The notice may be signed by a duly authorised agent, such as a solicitor or estate agent: *Tennant v London County Council* (1957) 121 JP 428.

'Substantially to the like effect'

In *Sabella Ltd v Montgomery* [1998] 1 EGLR 65, the Court of Appeal gave guidance on what 'substantially to the like effect' meant. The forms in that case differed in that they lacked some of the warning notices and omitted some of the paragraphs. It was held that:

- the comparison to be made is between the notices served and the form;
- it is immaterial that any addition or omission had no material effect upon the actual recipient;
- once the differences have been ascertained, then the decision as to whether the two are substantially to like effect will depend upon the importance of the differences rather than their number or amount;
- a difference can only be disregarded when the information given as to the particular recipient's rights and obligations under the LTA 1954 is in substance as effective as that set out in the form;
- a matter that is irrelevant to the recipient's rights or obligations may be omitted as in such a case the notice has given to the recipient information substantially to like effect as that in the form.

Specifying the property comprised in the notice

- The notice must specify the premises to which the notice relates. A minor error will not invalidate the notice, but in *Herongrove Limited v Wates City of London Properties* [1988] 1 EGLR 82 a failure to refer to a basement car park invalidated the notice.
- It is recommended that the author of the notice quotes the actual definition given in the lease, and then specifically refers to the lease itself.
- Even where the tenant's holding is less than the whole of the tenancy, the section 25 notice must relate to the whole of the

tenancy: *Eastern Power Networks plc (formerly EDF Energy Networks) (EPN plc) v BOH Ltd* [2011] EWCA Civ 19.

Timing

A section 25 Notice is invalid unless it is given (a) not more than 12 months and (b) not less than 6 months, before the termination date given: section 25(2).

The notice must not, however, give a date that is earlier than when the contractual period of the tenancy will finish:

- Where the tenancy can be brought to an end by way of a notice to quit given by the landlord, the date of termination in the notice must not be earlier than the earlier date that the tenancy could have been brought to an end by a notice to quit given by the landlord on the day that the section 25 notice is given (section 25(3)(a) LTA 1954);

- Where more than six months' notice to quit is required to bring the tenancy to an end, section 25(3)(a) is modified so that instead of an 'upper limit' of 12 months, the upper limit on the timing is a period six months longer than the length of the notice to quit which would have been required. (for example, if the contractual notice period is 12 months, the notice must be served not less than 12 months but not more than 18 months before the date of termination). (LTA 1954, section 25(3)(b)).

A section 25 Notice must not specify date of termination earlier than the date when the contractual tenancy would have come to an end by effluxion of time: section 25(4) LTA 1954. This is particularly relevant where a landlord is serving a section 25 Notice on the tenant of a fixed term tenancy.

Must identify the competent parties

It is important to identify the parties accurately. In *Yamaha-Kemble Music (UK) Ltd v ARC Properties Ltd* [1990] 1 EGLR 261, the section 25 Notice named the defendant itself, ARC Properties Ltd, as landlords. Unfortunately, shortly before this notice was served the landlord's interest had been assigned to ARC Property Developments Ltd, the parent company. The defendant argued that this was a case of misnomer, so that the correct landlord could be read on to the notice. Aldous J disagreed: 'It may be that misdescriptions of a landlord will not invalidate a section 25 notice, but in this case there is no doubt that the wrong company was named as the landlord.' He referred to *Morrow v Nadeem* [1986] 1 WLR 1381, where Nicholls LJ noted that there 'might perhaps be an exceptional case in which, notwithstanding the inadvertent misstatement or omission of the name of the landlord, any reasonable tenant would have known that that was a mistake and known clearly what was intended. But that is not this case.'

In *Dukeminster Ltd v West End Investments (Cowell Group) Ltd* (Central London County Court) [2019] L & TR 4, HHJ Saggerson held that a section 25 Notice which erroneously stated as the tenant a parent company rather than its similarly named subsidiary was valid in all the circumstances. Referring to *Morrow v Nadeem* and applying *Mannai Investment Co Ltd v Eagle Star Life Assurance Co Ltd* [1997] AC 749, it was held that the validity of the notice was to be objectively assessed: how, in the light of the mistake, would a reasonable person in the position of the recipient have understood the section 25 Notice. In the circumstances, a reasonable recipient would 'immediately and clearly' have understood the intended addressee of the notice to be the then actual tenant.

A section 25 Notice must be given by all the landlords. The omission of the name and address of one of the landlords renders the notice invalid for the purposes of the LTA 1954 and therefore ineffective to terminate the protected tenancy of the tenant under the Act: *Morrow v Nadeem* [1986] 1 WLR 1381.

The immediate landlord may not be 'competent' to serve a section 25 notice: see section 44 LTA 1954, which is discussed in chapter 2.

Where the tenancy is held by two or more persons, they comprise the tenant together: notice must be given to all of them (*Jacobs v Chaudhuri* [1968] 2 QB 470).

In the case of tenancies held by partnerships, however, do note the provisions of section 41A LTA 1954. This provision applies where:

a) a tenancy is held jointly by two or more persons (the joint tenants); and

b) the property comprised in the tenancy is or includes premises occupied for the purposes of a business; and

c) the business (or some other business) was at some time during the existence of the tenancy carried on in partnership by all the persons who were then the joint tenants or by those and other persons and the joint tenants' interest in the premises was then partnership property; and

d) the business is carried on (whether alone or in partnership with other persons) by one or some only of the joint tenants (who are called the business tenants) and no part of the property comprised in the tenancy is occupied, in right of the tenancy, for the purposes of a business carried on (whether alone or in partnership with other persons) by the other or others.

A notice given by the landlord to the business tenants which, had it been given to all the joint tenants, would have been a section 25 Notice shall be treated as such a notice, and references in that section to the tenant shall be construed accordingly (LTA 1954, section 41A(4)).

Opposition to a new lease?

A section 25 Notice must state whether a landlord is opposed to the grant of a new lease to the tenant: section 25(6) LTA 1954.

<u>Landlord not opposing new lease</u>

If the landlord is not opposing the grant of a new tenancy, the notice must contain the following information to be valid:

- the property to be comprised in the new tenancy (being either the whole or part of the property comprised in the current tenancy) (LTA 1954 section 25(8)(a));

- the rent to be payable under the new tenancy (LTA 1954 section 25(8)(b); and

- the other terms of the new tenancy. (LTA 1954 section 25(8)(c)).

It is possible to bring the current tenancy to an end (on its current terms) and for the landlord to agree to the grant of a new lease (on new terms). The section 25 Notice starts the timetable for the landlord and tenant to decide new terms or, if they cannot reach agreement, to have the court decide those terms.

Landlord opposing new lease

If the landlord opposes a new lease, he or she must specify the ground or grounds of opposition he or she is relying on under section 30(1) LTA 1954 in the section 25 notice. It is not possible to add new grounds later on: a landlord can only rely on those grounds specified in the notice (see, for example, *Nursey v P Currie (Dartford) Ltd* [1959] 1 WLR 273, where at 278 Wynn-Parry LJ held that there was no right of amendment).

Partially residential leases

Where part of the property comprised in the tenancy includes residential tenancies, you should be aware that it is possible that the Leasehold Reform Act 1967 might apply if the lease is a long lease of more than 35 years. If the LRA 1967 means that the tenant 'may' be entitled, and the landlord is opposed to the grant of a new tenancy under the LTA 1954, the prescribed form that should be used is Form 7: 'Ending a tenancy to which Part 2 of the Act applies, where the landlord is opposed to the grant of a new tenancy but where the tenant may be entitled under the 1967 Act to buy the freehold or an extended lease (notice under section 25 of the Act and paragraph 10 of Schedule 3 to the 1967 Act).'

Paragraph 10 of Schedule 3 of the LRA 1967 reads as follows:

> *(1) This paragraph shall have effect in relation to a landlord's notice terminating a tenancy of a house under section 4 or 25 of the Landlord and Tenant Act 1954 or under paragraph 4(1) of Schedule 10 to the Local Government and Housing Act 1989 if—*
>
> > *(a) no previous notice terminating the tenancy has been given under any of those provisions; and*

(b) in the case of a notice under section 25, the tenancy is a long tenancy at a low rent, and the tenant is not a company or other artificial person.

(2) The landlord's notice shall not have effect unless it states—

(a) that, if the tenant has a right under Part I of this Act to acquire the freehold or an extended lease of property comprised in the tenancy, notice of his desire to have the freehold or an extended lease cannot be given more than two months after the service of the landlord's notice; and

(b) that, in the event of a tenant having that right and giving such a notice within those two months, the landlord's notice will not operate; and

(c) that, in the event of the tenant giving such a notice within those two months, the landlord will be entitled to apply to the court under section 17 or 18 of this Act and proposes to do so or, as the case may be, will not be entitled or does not propose to do so.

(2A) If the landlord's notice is under section 25 of the Landlord and Tenant Act 1954, sub-paragraph (2) above shall effect in relation to it as if in paragraph (b), after the word "operate" there were inserted the words "and no further proceedings may be taken by him under Part 2 of the Landlord and Tenant Act 1954".

(3) The landlord shall also in the notice give the names and addresses of any other persons known or believed by him to have an interest superior to the tenancy terminated by the notice or to be the agent concerned with the property on behalf of a person having such an interest; and for this purpose "an interest superior to the tenancy terminated by the notice" means the estate in fee simple and any tenancy superior to that tenancy, but includes also a tenancy reversionary on that tenancy.

(4) Where a tenant's notice of his desire to have the freehold or an extended lease of a house and premises under Part I of this Act is given after the service of a landlord's notice terminating the tenancy under section 4 or section 25 of the Landlord and Tenant Act 1954 or under

> *paragraph 4(1) of Schedule 10 to the Local Government and Housing Act 1989, and the landlord's notice does not comply with sub-paragraph (2) above, no application made under section 17 or 18 of this Act with respect to the house and premises by the landlord giving the notice shall be entertained by the court (other than an application under section 17 after the grant of an extended lease).*

If, therefore, the tenant serves a notice under the LRA 1967 (and is entitled to do so) within two months of the section 25 notice, the section 25 Notice will not operate. On the other hand, the landlord will be able to serve a notice under section 16 or 17 LRA 1967.

CHECKLIST: section 25 Notice

- It must be given on the prescribed form, or a form substantially to the like effect.
- It must be given by the competent landlord (who might not be the immediate landlord).
- It must be given to the tenant.
- It must refer to the whole of the property in the tenancy.
- It must specify a date for termination which complies with the requirements BOTH of the LTA 1954 AND the lease itself.
- It must state if the landlord is opposing a new tenancy:
  - If a new tenancy is opposed, the statutory grounds upon which the landlord relies must be stated.
  - If the landlord does not oppose the grant of a new tenancy, it must contain the landlord's proposals as to (a) the property comprised in the tenancy (b) the rent (c) other terms.

Invalidity of the section 25 notice

If a section 25 Notice is invalid, a further section 25 Notice can be served (provided that the parties have not taken a step which would preclude such a notice being served, such as if the tenant serves a section 26 Notice).

Amendment or withdrawal of section 25 notices

It is not possible to amend or withdraw a section 25 Notice under the LTA 1954. The only exception to this is where the competent landlord has changed. Where the competent landlord has given a notice under section 25 to terminate the tenancy and, within two months after the giving of the notice, a superior landlord—

a) becomes the competent landlord; and

b) gives to the tenant notice in the prescribed form that he withdraws the notice previously given,

the section 25 Notice shall cease to have effect, but without prejudice to the giving of a further notice under that section by the competent landlord (LTA 1954, Schedule 6, para 6).

It is open to a landlord to abandon an invalid section 25 Notice.

While a landlord can abandon a ground of opposition, it is not possible to add a further ground.

Break notices

A section 25 Notice can sometimes perform 'double duty' as both a notice to activate a break clause and a section 25 notice as well: *Scholl Manufacturing Co. Ltd v Clifton (Slim-Line) Ltd* [1967] Ch 41. In that case there was a break clause on six months' notice. A section 25 Notice was sent by the landlord to the tenant. It was held that the section 25 Notice was sufficient to activate the break clause and that it was not necessary to serve a notice to bring the break clause into operation separately. It may not be possible to use a section 25 Notice to satisfy the contractual requirements of the lease, however. In practice, many landlords serve two notices.

The contractual tenancy has to be terminated on the same date as, or before, the date given in the section 25 Notice, otherwise the date specified in the section 25 Notice will be earlier than the earliest date on which the tenancy could have been terminated by notice to quit by the landlord. The validity of the section 25 Notice will therefore hinge on the fulfilment of the condition precedent to the exercise of the break clause. If a notice is served that satisfies section 25 but not the provisions of the break clause, the section 25 Notice will not take effect.

If the break clause is correctly triggered but the section 25 Notice is not effective, the contractual tenancy will be brought to an end but the tenancy itself will continue under section 24.

Split reversions

Where the reversion has become split after the grant of the tenancy all the reversioners must give the notice as the severance does not create separate tenancies. It is even possible for a tenant to become one of its own landlords and refuse to join in the service of a section 25 Notice: *Eastern Power Networks plc (formerly EDF Energy Networks) (EPN plc) v BOH Ltd* [2011] EWCA Civ 19.

Service of the section 25 notice

Section 23 of the Landlord and Tenant Act 1927 applies for the purposes of the LTA 1954 pursuant to section 66(4) LTA 1954.

> *Landlord and Tenant Act 1927: section 23 Service of notices*
>
> *(1) Any notice, request, demand or other instrument under this Act shall be in writing and may be served on the person on whom it is to be served either personally, or by leaving it for him at his last known place of abode* in England or Wales, or by sending it through the post in a registered letter addressed to him there, or, in the case of a local or public authority or a statutory or a public utility company, to the secretary or other proper officer at the principal office of such authority or company, and in the case of a notice to a landlord, the person on whom it is to be served shall include any agent of the landlord duly authorised in that behalf.*
>
> *(2) Unless or until a tenant of a holding shall have received notice that the person theretofore entitled to the rents and profits of the holding*

(hereinafter referred to as "the original landlord") has ceased to be so entitled, and also notice of the name and address of the person who has become entitled to such rents and profits, any claim, notice, request, demand, or other instrument, which the tenant shall serve upon or deliver to the original landlord shall be deemed to have been served upon or delivered to the landlord of such holding.

** A reference to a business is imported: Price v West London Investment Building Society [1964] 1 WLR 616*

If a permitted mode of service is used, then service is proved even if the document was not received by the intended recipient.

In *Stylo Shoes Ltd v Price Tailors Ltd* [1960] Ch 396, it was held that the requirements for service under section 23(1) LTA 1954 are satisfied if a letter containing the notice was delivered to and in fact received by the person to whom the notice was given.

See also Chapter 4 on service.

Subtenancies

The competent landlord can determine sub-tenancies as well with a section 25 Notice.

In *Lewis v M.T.C. (Cars) Ltd* [1975] 1 WLR 457, the freeholder (who was the competent landlord) served a section 25 Notice on the subtenant terminating the subtenancy before expiry of the mesne landlords' term. This was held to be acceptable: no fetter was imposed on the date of termination to be specified in the notice.

There is no difficulty in timing where two notices are given simultaneously (e.g. on both the tenant and the sub-tenant, where the party serving the notice would only become the competent landlord if the notice had been served on the mesne tenant before the notice served on the subtenant) as they are deemed to have been given in the appropriate order: *Keith Bailey Rogers & Co v Cubes Ltd* [1975] 31 P&CR 412.

Application for an order for termination

A landlord who has served a section 25 Notice opposing the grant of a new tenancy may apply to the court for an order for the termination of the tenancy without the grant of a new tenancy, provided that an application has not already been made by either the tenant or the landlord for a new tenancy.

Tied pubs

The Pubs Code etc Regulations 2016 regulations 15, 16, 17 and 18 introduce more detailed requirements as to the rent proposal where a landlord is serving a section 25 Notice on a tied pub tenant. Subject to those regulations, at the tenant's request the landlord must provide the prescribed information within a set timeframe.

Tenant's response

Service of a section 25 Notice precludes service of a section 26 Notice: section 26(4) LTA 1954.

It is no longer necessary for a tenant to serve a counter-notice in reply to a section 25 Notice. If the tenant wishes to renew his or her tenancy, he or she must either agree a new tenancy with the landlord (Chapter 21) or apply to the court for a new tenancy (Chapter 23). It is possible to agree an extension of time to make the application with the landlord: section 29B LTA 1954.

Where an agreement is made under section 29B, or two or more agreements are made under that provision, the section 25 Notice shall be treated as terminating the tenancy at the end of the period specified in the agreement or, as the case may be, at the end of the period specified in the last of those agreements (section 29B(4) LTA 1954).

Notice to terminate a tenancy that is no longer protected by the LTA 1954

Tenancy ceases to be protected

A tenancy may cease being protected by the LTA 1954 e.g. if the tenant stops carrying on a business in the premises. When this happens, section 24(3)(a) confirms that the tenancy shall not come to an end only because it now falls outside the protection of the LTA 1954. If the tenant was granted for a term of years certain and has been continued by section 24(1) then (without prejudice to termination in accordance with any terms of the tenancy) it may be terminated by notice in writing given by the landlord to the tenant. There must be not less than three nor more than six months' notice.

Tenancy becomes protected after landlord's notice to quit

Where a landlord gives notice to quit when the tenancy is not protected by the LTA 1954, the notice is not be affected if the tenancy becomes one to which this Part of this Act applies after the giving of the notice: section 24(3)(b) LTA 1954.

CHAPTER ELEVEN

THE GROUNDS OF OPPOSITION TO THE GRANT OF A NEW LEASE TO THE TENANT

As we have seen, there are a number of procedural ways that the question of whether the tenant should be granted a new tenancy can come before the Court. Whether the issue arises as a result of a tenant's claim for a new tenancy following either (a) the service of a Section 25 Notice by the landlord, (b) a section 26 request by the tenant or (c) a landlord's claim for termination following its service of a Section 25 Notice, the grounds upon which the landlord can resist the grant of a new tenancy are the same. The seven grounds are set out in section 30 (1) (a) to (g) of the LTA 1954, which is a complete code setting out the only grounds on which the landlord can rely.

The grounds of opposition on which a landlord may oppose an application for a new lease under section 24(1) LTA 1954 or make an application under section 29(2) LTA 1954 are listed in section 30(1).

> *a. where under the current tenancy the tenant has any obligations as respects the repair and maintenance of the holding, that the tenant ought not to be granted a new tenancy in view of the state of repair of the holding, being a state resulting from the tenant's failure to comply with the said obligations;*
>
> *b. that the tenant ought not to be granted a new tenancy in view of his persistent delay in paying rent which has become due;*
>
> *c. that the tenant ought not to be granted a new tenancy in view of other substantial breaches by him of his obligations under the current tenancy, or for any other reason connected with the tenant's use or management of the holding;*
>
> *d. that the landlord has offered and is willing to provide or secure the provision of alternative accommodation for the tenant, that the terms*

on which the alternative accommodation is available are reasonable having regard to the terms of the current tenancy and to all other relevant circumstances, and that the accommodation and the time at which it will be available are suitable for the tenant's requirements (including the requirement to preserve goodwill) having regard to the nature and class of his business and to the situation and extent of, and facilities afforded by, the holding;

e. where the current tenancy was created by the sub-letting of part only of the property comprised in a superior tenancy and the landlord is the owner of an interest in reversion expectant on the termination of that superior tenancy, that the aggregate of the rents reasonably obtainable on separate lettings of the holding and the remainder of that property would be substantially less than the rent reasonably obtainable on a letting of that property as a whole, that on the termination of the current tenancy the landlord requires possession of the holding for the purpose of letting or otherwise disposing of the said property as a whole, and that in view thereof the tenant ought not to be granted a new tenancy;

f. that on the termination of the current tenancy the landlord intends to demolish or reconstruct the premises comprised in the holding or a substantial part of those premises or to carry out substantial work of construction on the holding or part thereof and that he could not reasonably do so without obtaining possession of the holding;

g. subject as hereinafter provided, that on the termination of the current tenancy the landlord intends to occupy the holding for the purposes, or partly for the purposes, of a business to be carried on by him therein, or as his residence.

Some of the grounds are discretionary, that is, even if they are established, the court possesses a discretion not to order possession. The discretionary grounds are grounds A, B, C, and E. Grounds D, F and G are not discretionary: if the court finds that the statutory criteria are made out it has no choice but to order possession.

Further, some of the grounds (the so-called 'no fault' grounds) entitle a tenant to statutory compensation (discussed in chapter 19): these are grounds E, F and G. It should be noted that ground D does not entitle a tenant to compensation, even though no fault needs to be shown on the part of the tenant.

A Section 25 Notice cannot be amended, although grounds specified in the notice can be abandoned. The landlord would be best advised, therefore, to include all properly arguable *bona fide* grounds that either it or a successor in title might properly wish to deploy at trial.

It is also necessary to keep an eye to the fact that, in certain factual circumstances, the competent landlord might change between service of a Section 25 Notice (or counter notice to a tenant's Section 26 Notice) and trial. So, landlord A might be the competent landlord at the date of service of (say) a Hostile Section 25 Notice, whereas landlord B might be the competent landlord by the time of the trial. In such a case, landlord B will be bound by, and need to rely upon, the notice served by landlord A. It is therefore important that when landlord A drafts its notice it considers whether there are any additional grounds which landlord B might properly wish to rely upon at trial; this is particularly important as regards Grounds F (redevelopment) and G (landlord wishing to occupy).

Because of the differences between the various grounds in relation to whether compensation is or is not payable, there is sometimes a temptation for a landlord who has a decent ground of opposition on a ground that *would* attract compensation (say Ground F) to spuriously include in addition a ground that would *not* attract compensation (say Ground A). This should be avoided as the law appears to be that the landlord is required to act *bona fide* in specifying the grounds of opposition to a new tenancy and the inclusion of a ground in bad faith would most likely invalidate the whole notice: see, in particular, the dicta of Lord Denning in *Betty's Cafes v Phillips Furnishing Stores* [1959] A.C. 20 at page 52; see also *Morris Marks v British Waterways Board* [1963] 1 WLR 1008 and *Sevenarts v Bursive* [1968] 1 WLR 1921). Satellite battles on the efficacy of notices are to be avoided if possible, not least because of the possible cost consequences and delay.

We adopt the convention often used in practice of referring to the various alphabetic sub-sections of section 30(1) as "**Grounds**"; all bold in quotations in quoting the statutory text is our emphasis.

Possession obtained by misrepresentation and/or concealment

Section 37(A) LTA 1954 provides that the court may order the landlord to pay the tenant compensation where either (1) the court had refused to grant a new tenancy or (2) the tenant has decided not to pursue, or not to make, a claim for a new tenancy by reason of a misrepresentation or concealment of material facts. In either case, the compensation is to be in respect of damage or loss sustained by the tenant as a result of quitting the holding.

Section 37(A) LTA 1954 was introduced by the 2003 Order and expands the scope of the former section 55 (which it replaces) by encompassing the scenarios where the tenant decided not to make or pursue an application. The text below deals with the position for tenants who quit after the coming into force of the 2004 Order; the old section 55 should be consulted for tenants who quit before that date.

The section does not say in terms by whom the misrepresentation, or concealment, has to be made; presumably, however, it must be by the landlord or its agent.

The provisions are most likely to be engaged in a Ground F or G case. The landlord needs to take care not to make any statements which could later be relied on by the tenant as misrepresentations. The case of *Inclusive Technology v Williamson* [2009] EWCA Civ 718 is particularly instructive in this regard: the landlord had served a Section 25 Notice specifying Ground F but subsequently changed its mind as regards development, deciding to postpone its plans but not sharing that decision with its tenant which moved out to more expensive premises in the interim and then sued for compensation under section 37A LTA 1954 on discovering that the works had not been carried out. The Court of Appeal (strictly speaking, *obiter*) considered that the service of a Section 25 Notice specifying Ground F *in itself* did not constitute a statement capable of constituting a representation. However, the landlord had served the notice under a covering letter which also set out its plans for redevelopment; there had, also, been a series of discussions between the parties in the lead up to service of the notice. The Court of Appeal decided that the covering letter constituted a representation as to the landlord's intentions – and that the statutory context was such that the representation was a continuing representation which the landlord should have corrected once its plans changed.

The Court of Appeal was of the view, however, that there was no requirement for a running commentary by the landlord as to its intentions and that a continuing representation would not be rendered false '...simply because the landlord explored other commercial options...' [per Hughes LJ at para 34]. Drawing the line as to when the landlord's change of intent comes about, however, and when the line is crossed can be difficult.

Although one reaction to the decision in *Inclusive Technology* might be to consider keeping communication to a minimum – and simply serving a Section 25 Notice shorn of any associated correspondence this would appear to be somewhat unrealistic. Reasonable pre-action behaviour dictates that a landlord engages. The better stance, therefore, is to be alive to the need to correct any representations if the landlord's intentions change.

CHAPTER TWELVE
GROUND A – TENANT'S DISREPAIR

> *"where under the current tenancy the tenant has any obligations as respects the* ***repair and maintenance*** *of the* ***holding****, that the tenant* ***ought not*** *to be granted a new tenancy in view of the* ***state of repair*** *of the* ***holding****, being a state resulting from the tenant's failure to comply with the said obligations" (bold here and in other quoted sections of the Grounds is our emphasis.)*

Like Grounds B and C, Ground A involves a two-stage process.

First, the necessary factual trigger needs to be established: here, under Ground A, that trigger is a certain state of repair of the holding resulting from a failure to comply with repair/maintenance obligations.

Secondly, once the trigger has been established, the court goes on to consider whether the tenant 'ought not to be granted a tenancy'. The second stage imports a degree of discretion (albeit, to be exercised judicially in line with principle); in *Horne & Meredith Properties Ltd v Cox and another* [2014] 2 P & CR 297, a case under Ground C, Lewison LJ preferred to describe the second stage as a "value judgment" as opposed to the exercise of a "discretion". Whichever description of the exercise one takes, it would appear that an appeal court will be slow to interfere with a first instance judge's application of the second stage, providing there has not been an error of principle.

As regards the first stage, it is important to note that the focus under Ground A, both in terms of obligations and condition, is on '*the holding*'.

> '*The holding*" is defined by section 23 (3) of the Act as meaning "*...the property comprised in the tenancy, there being excluded any part thereof which is occupied neither by the tenant nor by any person employed by the tenant and so employed for the purposes of a business by reason of which the tenancy is one to which this Part of this Act applies*'.

So, if (say) the tenant has sublet part of the demised premises and it is the sub-let part which is in disrepair, the landlord could not rely on Ground A in relation to that want of repair. (Consider, perhaps, whether such a matter could be pursued under Ground C in such a case). See also chapter 2 for further discussion of 'the holding'.

The want of repair required has to be 'substantial': *per* Ormrod LJ in *Lyons v Central Commercial Properties Ltd* [1958] 1 WLR 869. In *Youssefi v Musselwhite* [2014] 2 P & CR 14, a case under Grounds A, B and C, Gloster LJ utilised the cost of repair, put at £350, in deciding alleged want of repair would not have been substantial.

At what point in time must the want of repair be shown? As will be seen below, *Betty's Cafes v Phillips Furnishing Stores* [1959] AC 20 is the leading case on the relevant date for ascertaining the landlord's intentions under Ground F. In that case, certain members of the House of Lords also considered, *obiter*, the timing for establishing other grounds including A, B and C. Viscount Simonds suggested that '*it is not to be supposed*' that a landlord would include Ground A unless there were repair issues at the date of the section 25 Notice: '[the landlord] *will state that he will rely on ground (a) if and only if at the date of notice it gives him solid support. At the hearing the judge, whose power to grant a new tenancy is discretionary where this ground of opposition is pleaded, will necessarily take into consideration the state of repair or disrepair, not only at the date of notice, but also at the date of hearing.*' Indeed, assuming the need for a notice to be given in good faith, it is a little difficult to see how a landlord could specify Ground A unless there were repair issues at that date.

Assuming that the landlord makes out the first stage, what factors are to be considered in deciding whether the tenant 'ought not to' be granted a new tenancy? In particular, is the landlord confined to relying on the repair issues or can other, wider, breaches or considerations be taken into account?

In *Youssefi,* Gloster LJ suggested (albeit, strictly speaking, *obiter)* at paragraph 29 that the court was confined, under Ground A, to focus at the second stage '*exclusively on the state of repair*', rather than consider other, more general discretionary factors. For Gloster LJ the question was:

> '*...whether, looking forward to the hypothetical new term, 'the proper interests of the landlord would be prejudiced' by continuing in a landlord/tenant relationship with this particular tenant ......or, put another way, whether it 'would be unfair to the landlord', having regard to the tenant's past performances and behaviour in relation to its obligations to repair and maintain the holding, if the tenant were to be 'foisted on the landlord for a new term'....*' [The two quotations were from *John Kay Ltd v Kay* [1952] 2 QB 258 and *Lyons v Central Commercial Properties (London) Ltd* [1958] 1 WLR 869 respectively: Gloster LJ considered there were only semantic differences between the two approaches and, in reality, they amounted to the same thing].

There has been some doubt cast as to whether *Youseffi* is correct in suggesting that the Court is confined at the discretionary stage in the manner described immediately above, as opposed to being able to consider much broader discretionary matters such as other breaches or tenant conduct. See, for example, the discussion by Caroline Shea QC in the Estates Gazette, 4th March 2017, in which it is noted that the Court of Appeal decision in *Hutchinson v Lambert* [1984] 1 EGLR 75 appears not to have been cited in *Yousseffi*. *Hutchinson*, albeit a case under Ground B, decided that broader circumstances *could* be considered at the discretionary stage. (The article discusses the first instance County Court decision of HHJ Baucher, 8 February 2017 in *Norfolk Square (Northern Section) Ltd v M&P Enterprises*, as yet unreported, in which the learned Judge appears to have followed *Yousseffi* as regards Ground A, distinguishing and confining the *Hutchinson* decision to Ground B. This outcome is not entirely satisfactory as the relevant wording of Grounds A, B and C in relation to discretion – '*ought not to*' – is the same and one might expect a consistent interpretation of the statutory language). (An appeal, not against the judgment itself or any of the specific findings, rather, that the process underlying the judgment was so unfair as to render its outcome void, was dismissed: [2018] EWHC 2665 (Ch).

If *Yousseffi* is correct on this point and the focus under Ground A at the discretionary stage is confined to repair/maintenance, rather than taking in wider discretionary factors and other breaches, then this marks up the importance of the landlord considering carefully at the notice stage whether to include additional grounds in an appropriate case (*e.g.* Grounds B and/or C if they could *bona fide* be made out).

The landlord does not need to show any diminution in value of its reversion as a result of the want of repair/maintenance to succeed under Ground A (nor, indeed, B or C): *Youseffi* at para 30.

Practical Tactics

It is considered the following points are worthy of consideration:

a) In the run up to a renewal a landlord may wish to consider holding back the service of a schedule of dilapidations so as to limit the time the tenant has to respond.

b) If acting for the tenant in relation to premises that are in poor repair, the opportunity to right matters between service of the notice and the hearing ought to be taken as best as possible; see the discussion referred to above in *Betty's Cafes* regarding the premises being put into repair by the date of the hearing.

c) If the premises cannot be put into repair by the date of the hearing, then the tenant should consider volunteering a schedule of works to be carried out. (Indeed, if a lease *is* to be granted, there are certain procedural advantages to a landlord in such a schedule being included within the new lease itself.)

d) If past conduct is particularly bad, and/or the tenant's credibility is likely to be regarded as poor, then means of demonstrating the proposed works are a reality, rather than an empty promise, should be considered. Evidence as to contractors being engaged (if only on a conditional/contingent basis) would be helpful, as would evidence that the works have been properly costed and can be funded.

e) If there are broader, and genuine, matters relating to other tenant breaches then given the discussion above regarding *Yousseffi,* serious consideration should be given to including Ground B (if the breach is in relation to payment of rent) or Ground C.

f) Although evidence as to diminution in value is unnecessary following *Youssefi*, if the landlord can obtain it (and it is not a hostage to fortune), consideration may be given to deploying that as icing on the cake.

CHAPTER THIRTEEN

GROUND B – PERSISTENT DELAY IN PAYING RENT

> "*that the tenant* ***ought not*** *to be granted a new tenancy in view of his* ***persistent delay*** *in paying* ***rent*** *which has become due*"

The points made above under Ground A apply: namely, there is a two stage process. The first stage requires the factual trigger to be established, namely persistent delay in paying rent that has become due. The second stage engages a discretion/value judgment as to whether the tenant "ought" to be granted a new tenancy.

As regards the width of the discretion once the first stage trigger is satisfied, the Court of Appeal suggested, *obiter*, in *Yousseffi,* that under Ground B the discretion should be focused exclusively on the persistent delay in paying rent and nothing else, *i.e.* wider discretionary factors could not be considered. However, this would appear to be in direct conflict with the earlier Court of Appeal decision in *Hutchinson* which was a Ground B case and does not appear to have been cited in *Youssefi* (see the general discussion in this regard under Ground A, above).

The delay in paying needs to be in respect of 'rent which has become due'. Many leases reserve other sums, such as insurance premiums or service charges, as rent. It is arguable that the term 'rent' should extend to payment of these sums (following *Escalus Properties Ltd v Robinson* [1996] QB 231, where the Court of Appeal held that sums reserved as rent invested them with the character of rent for the purpose of section 138 of the County Courts Act 1984 and section 38 of the Supreme Court Act 1981), although there does not appear to be any authority on the point.

A landlord can become estopped from contending that rent is lawfully due: *Hazel v Akhtar* [2002] 1 EGLR 45. So if, say, by concession the landlord agrees that rent payable quarterly in advance can instead be paid monthly in arrears and the parties operate the lease on that basis then it seems unlikely that the landlord would be unable to rely on that conduct until such time as he has given notice to terminate the arrangement.

'Persistent' would appear to connote either a considerable delay in making one payment or, much more compellingly, repeated failures to pay. The inconvenience and effects of late payment on the landlord may be relevant, as will the reasons for late payment.

To avoid the suggestion that the landlord is acquiescing in late payment, a landlord may consider protecting itself by corresponding with its tenant making it plain that payment in accordance with the strict terms of the lease is required.

If advising the tenant and faced with a difficult/marginal case it may be worth considering offering a rent deposit or other forms of security.

Coronavirus Act 2020

By section 82(11) of the Coronavirus Act 2020, for the purpose of determining whether Ground B is established, any failure to pay rent under that tenancy during the *"relevant period"* is disregarded. The relevant period began on 26 March 2020, the day after the 2020 Act was passed; the end of the relevant period under section 82(12) is set by a statutory instrument (which, at the time of writing, ended the period on 30 June 2021 under the Business Tenancies (Protection from Forfeiture: Relevant Period) (Coronavirus) (England) Regulations 2021 (S.I. 2021/283), regulation 2).

CHAPTER FOURTEEN

GROUND C – TENANT'S SUBSTANTIAL BREACHES

> "*that the tenant* ***ought not*** *to be granted a new tenancy in view of other* ***substantial*** *breaches by him of his* ***obligations under the current tenancy****, or* ***for any other reason connected with the tenant's use or management of the holding***"

This Ground, again, adopts the two stage approach: first, the factual trigger (which, in this case contains two alternative limbs) and secondly the discretionary / value judgment stage.

The factual trigger stage divides in two and the landlord may satisfy either:

a) substantial breaches by the tenant of obligations under the current tenancy; or

b) any other reason connected with the tenant's use or management of the holding.

It is worth noting that the 'substantial breaches' limb does not require the breach of obligation to relate to '*the holding*'; so it could, presumably, relate to property within the demise which has been sub-let. It is also worth noting, by contrast, that the "*any other reason*" limb *is* confined to the holding but is *not* confined to breaches.

The Court of Appeal usefully considered Ground C in *Horne & Meredith Properties Ltd v Cox and another* [2014] 2 P & CR 297 which was a case where the relationship between the parties had broken down. The facts were somewhat extreme: there had been extensive previous litigation between the parties, with considerable cost consequences, and the tenant had been the subject of a civil restraint order. The Court of Appeal (relying on *Eichner v Midland and Trustee Company Ltd* [1970] 1 WLR 1120) took the view that the prolonged history of vexatious litigation between the parties, in respect of a right of way demised under the lease, was a matter connected with the use and management of the holding.

Lewison LJ, with whom Sir Stanley Burton and Ryder LJ agreed, considered in *Horne* that (at [27]):

> *The phrase 'ought not' does to my mind suggest that there should usually be some fault or culpability on the part of the tenant* (underlining my emphasis).

He also considered (at [27]) that:

> *If the landlord had been the aggressor in the litigation or if the tenant's litigation has been responsibly and proportionately conducted the answer to that question [i.e. whether the tenant should be refused a new tenancy] may well be no.*

It is to be noted that both quotations appear to admit of the *possibility* that a non-aggressor tenant who is in no way at fault for the litigation could, conceptually, fall foul of Ground C. That said, it strikes the writer that any such case would be extremely difficult to pursue, and unattractive.

Other circumstances in which Ground C have operated include:

1) where the use of the holding would breach planning control (*Turner & Bell v Searles (Stanford -le-Hope) Ltd* (1977) 33 P & CR 208); and

2) where the tenant's business depended on him living proximately to the demised premises and his living arrangements were regarded as being too precarious (*Beard v Williams* [1986] 1 EGLR 148).

CHAPTER FIFTEEN

GROUND D – SUITABLE ALTERNATIVE ACCOMMODATION

> *(d) that* ***the landlord has offered and is willing to provide or secure the provision of alternative accommodation for the tenant****, that the terms on which the alternative accommodation is available are reasonable having regard to the terms of the current tenancy and to all other relevant circumstances, and that* ***the accommodation and the time at which it will be available are suitable for the tenant's requirements*** *(including the requirement to preserve goodwill) having regard to the nature and class of his business and to the situation and extent of, and facilities afforded by, the holding*

The wording of this ground of opposition states that the alternative accommodation must:

- be reasonable having regard to the terms of the current tenancy;
- be reasonable in the light of all other relevant circumstances;
- be suitable for the tenant's requirements (including the requirement to preserve goodwill), having regard to:
  - the nature and class of his or her business;
  - the situation, size, and facilities of the holding.

Beyond this, there is considerable uncertainty in the wording of ground D. There are few reported cases about this ground to clarify its meaning.

There are similarities in the wording to the analogous ground adopted in the Rent Acts: see, for example, para 1 of Schedule 16, Rent Act 1977: 'The court is satisfied that suitable alternative accommodation is available for the tenant, or will be available for him when the order for possession takes effect.' Historically, however, this has been of little assistance to landlords, as the principles applicable to a residential tenancy have very little bearing on the position of a tenant who requires a place to conduct his or her business (for example, see *MacDonnell v Daly* [1969] 1 WLR 1482, where the residential tenant had professional needs as well and used the premises partly for professional purposes: little principled guidance was given by the Court of Appeal, however, as the case turned on the facts).

When must the offer be made?

It is not clear if the landlord must make an offer prior to, or at the time of, service of the section 25 Notice, and whether that he or she is fixed with that offer, or if the court hearing the preliminary issue can take into account improved offers by the landlord. HHJ Aron Owen, sitting in the Clerkenwell County Court, held in *M Chaplin Ltd v Regent Capital Holdings Ltd* [1994] 1 EGLR 249 that the landlord is fixed with the property he or she has offered before 'battle is joined', that is, before the issues are joined in the pleadings. In *Mark Stone Car Sales Ltd v Howard de Walden Estates Ltd* (1997) 733 P&CR D43, it was assumed, however, that it was a possibility that the judge might be able consider the terms of an improved offer made by the landlords before the end of the trial (subject to costs issues).

The tense of the first sentence ('the landlord has offered') suggests that the offer to the tenant was made before the service of the section 25 Notice. However, the landlord must show that the alternative accommodation will be available at the date of the hearing or when the tenancy terminates: *Betty's Cafés Ltd v Phillips Furnishing Stores Ltd* [1959] AC 20 at 34-35.

Offering part of existing accommodation

It is possible for the landlord to offer part of existing accommodation. However, the landlord must still show it is suitable for the tenant's requirements having regard to the nature and class of his business. In *Singh v Malayan Theatres* [1953] AC 632, a Privy Council case from Singapore, it was held that the landlord must show that there is alternative accommodation for the business carried on in those premises, not simply accommodation for carrying on the business of the statutory tenant in some different and diminished way by some kind of rearrangement in the mode of its conduct. It must be shown that the business carried on in those premises can be adequately carried on elsewhere.

Not sufficient to show that there are alternative properties in the marketplace

It is not sufficient for the landlord to provide particulars of alternative properties to show that there are appropriate lettings in the marketplace. Ground D, by its wording ('has offered and is willing to provide or secure') makes it clear that the landlord must be willing to provide, or secure the provision, of the alternative property.

Fixtures and fittings

The legislation itself is silent as to whether the fit-out costs of the alternative accommodation are part of the test. The tenant's fixtures and fittings do not form part of 'the holding', which is the relevant test for Ground D: *Knollys House v Sayer* [2006] PLSCS 55. However, matters such as goodwill are relevant to the statutory exercise, which refers to the 'alternative accommodation' as opposed to alternative letting.

CHAPTER SIXTEEN
GROUND E – SUBLETTING

"where the current tenancy was created by the sub-letting of part only of the property comprised in a superior tenancy and the landlord is the owner of an interest in reversion expectant on the termination of that superior tenancy, that the aggregate of the rents reasonably obtainable on separate lettings of the holding and the remainder of that property would be substantially less than the rent reasonably obtainable on a letting of that property as a whole, that on the termination of the current tenancy the landlord requires possession of the holding for the purpose of letting or otherwise disposing of the said property as a whole, and that in view thereof the tenant ***ought not*** *to be granted a new tenancy."*

This Ground appears to be very rarely used in practice.

The Ground requires:

a) A letting of property ('the Property') by a landlord ('L') to tenant ('T');

b) An underletting *of part* of that Property by T to a sub-tenant ('ST');

c) L to be the competent landlord of ST;

d) The aggregate of rents reasonably obtainable on separate lettings of (1) ST's holding and (2) the remainder of the property comprised in *the superior tenancy* to be "substantially less" than the rent reasonably obtainable on a letting of the property comprised in the superior tenancy as a whole.

e) It is difficult to see how the exercise at (d) could be carried out without expert evidence concerning valuation. Although the section is silent on the matter, the appropriate date for these valuations is probably the date of the hearing. (Reynolds & Clark are of this view at 7-91 of Renewal of Business Tenancies, 5th Edition)

f) L is required to show possession of ST's holding at the end of ST's tenancy is required for letting (or otherwise disposing) of the property as a whole. Presumably 'the property' means the whole of the Property which had been demised within the superior tenancy.

g) That as a matter of discretion/value judgment a new tenancy therefore 'ought not' to be granted to ST.

(We adopt the above definitions for the remainder of this section of the text).

It will be apparent that the factual scenario above will rarely be in play: it requires the residue of the intermediate tenancy (T's tenancy) to be sufficiently small to render the superior landlord ('L') the competent landlord of ST(*i.e.* 'landlord' within the meaning of section 44). Additionally, for L to be able to demonstrate that a new tenancy ought not to be granted to ST on the basis that a letting (or other disposal) of the whole will take place, L would need to demonstrate such a transaction could take place (presumably within a sensibly proximate period of time following the obtaining of possession). It seems likely, therefore, that the ground could only apply if T's tenancy did not enjoy Part II protection under the Act, or if L could demonstrate that tenancy would somehow otherwise be brought to an end.

There is little authority on the dates at which the various criteria need to be established. However, the superior tenancy has to be in existence at the date L gives the section 25 Notice: *Greaves v Stanhope* (1973) 228 EG 725. Whether that must also be the case *at the date of the hearing* would appear not to have been decided. The strict wording of the ground suggests this may well be the case but if this is so then the factual scenarios in which the ground could apply would be narrowed further because of the need to show L will be in a position to dispose of the property as a whole.

CHAPTER SEVENTEEN
GROUND F – LANDLORD INTENDS TO DEMOLISH OR RECONSTRUCT THE PREMISES

(f) that on the termination of the current tenancy the ***landlord intends to demolish or reconstruct the premises comprised in the holding or a substantial part of those premises*** *or to* ***carry out substantial work of construction on the holding*** *or part thereof and that he could not reasonably do so without obtaining possession of the holding*

This ground of opposition can be broken down as follows:

- the landlord 'intends'
- to 'demolish or reconstruct the premises comprised in the holding or a substantial part of those premises'
- or to 'carry out substantial work of construction on the holding or part thereof'
- the landlord 'could not reasonably do so without obtaining possession of the holding'.

Intention

Intention was defined in *Cunliffe v Goodman* [1950] 2 KB 237;

An 'intention' to my mind connotes a state of affairs which the party 'intending' – I will call him X – does more than merely contemplate: it connotes a state of affairs which, on the contrary, he decides, so far as in him lies, to bring about, and which, in point of possibility, he has a reasonable prospect of being able to bring about, by his own act of volition. X cannot, with any due regard to the English language, be said to 'intend' a result which is wholly beyond the control of his will.

The intention must be firm and settled, not likely to be changed (*Fisher v Taylors Furnishings Stores* [1956] 2 QB 78) and have moved out of the area of contemplation.

The Supreme Court in *S Franses Ltd v Cavendish Hotel (London) Ltd* [2018] UKSC 62 confirmed at [8] and [19]that there are two limbs to intention:

1) Genuine intention to carry out the qualifying works: the landlord must have a fixed and settled intention to actually carry out the works as at the time of the hearing, and

2) Practically able to do so: the landlord must have a reasonable prospect of being able to implement it (as opposed to the higher test of its being able to do this on the balance of probabilities: *Gregson v Cyril Lord* [1963] 1 WLR 41).

There is no principle or practice, however, that requires the two limbs to be dealt with sequentially. The first element of the subjective intention, the genuine settled commitment to the project, and the second is a 'check on reality' which is demonstrated by showing, objectively, that there is the real possibility of carrying it out: *Zarvos v Pradhan* [2003] EWCA Civ 208; [2003] 2 P&CR 9. In that case, it was held at para 45 that a judge must make it plain if he or she was rejecting the landlord's evidence: 'If that is his finding, he should make it plain that he does not believe him and, wherever possible, should explain why he does not believe him.' (*per* Ward LJ). This was confirmed by the Court of Appeal in *The Gulf Agencies Limited v Abdul Salam Seid Ahmed* [2016] EWCA Civ 44, [2016] 2 P. & C.R. DG1, which confirmed the need for the first instance court make clear findings as to the first limb of the test of intent.

The landlord's intention must be established at the time of the hearing: *Betty's Cafés Ltd v Phillips Furnishing Stores Ltd* [1959] AC 20. A subsequent landlord can rely upon its predecessor's section 25 Notice: *Marks v British Waterways Board* [1963] 1 WLR 1008, where it was held that a landlord's counter-notice opposing the grant of a new tenancy which was then relied on by a subsequent landlord was sufficient so long as it informed applicant for the new tenancy of the case which he would have to meet at the hearing of the application and was not fraudulent or deceptive or misleading.

Fixed and settled intention

It can be deceptively simple to prove this limb: at one level, it is sufficient simply to call the individual landlord to give evidence on oath. There is no strict need for corroboration: *Mirza v Nicola* [1990] 2 EGLR 73. On the other hand, if there is no corroborative evidence (*e.g.* steps taken towards redevelopment) the landlord's evidence alone might be somewhat lightweight.

Where 'the landlord is a limited company, the existence of the intention (and particularly the proof of the quality of the intention, that it is firm and settled) can be established only through the directors or other principal officers of the company' (*Fleet Electrics v Jacey Investments* [1956] 1 WLR 1027). What is sufficient will depend on the constitution of the company. In *Manchester City Garages Ltd v Petrofina (UK) Ltd* [1975] 1 EGLR 62 it was sufficient for a regional manager to give evidence of the company's intention.

In the past, some landlords have come up with contrived schemes in order to satisfy either Ground F or Ground G either solely or principally with the intent of obtaining possession of the holding. The question in the Supreme Court case of *S Franses Ltd v Cavendish Hotel (London) Ltd* [2018] UKSC 62 was a stark one: is it open to a landlord to oppose the grant of a new tenancy if the works which he says that he intends to carry out have no purpose other than to get rid of the tenant and would not be undertaken if the tenant were to leave voluntarily. The County Court judge had answered that question in the affirmative; that was reversed on a leap-frog appeal to the Supreme Court. The landlord's motive and purpose was not directly relevant; however if the primary purpose of the work is to get rid of the tenant, that can well undermine intention, particularly if there is no other point to the works. The Supreme Court stated that the landlord's intention to demolish or reconstruct the premises must exist independently of the tenant's statutory claim to a new tenancy. Lord Sumption stated that, "*The acid test is whether the landlord would intend to do the same works if the tenant left voluntarily.*" If they did not, then the landlord's intent was only conditional, and did not satisfy Ground F.

If the landlord intends to carry out only some parts of the works if the tenant left voluntarily, but has included extra works so as to make out

Ground F, then the tenant's claim to a new tenancy would be resolved by reference only to the works that the landlord unconditionally intends to carry out, whether or not the tenant vacates voluntarily. It is likely that this court of case will give rise to delicate and complicated questions of fact.

Following *Franses*, the court will therefore test the landlord's purpose or motive behind carrying out the works. The Supreme Court stated that the only legitimate purpose behind examining the landlord's purpose (beyond testing the genuineness of the landlord' intention) is to enable the court to decide if the landlord would have done the relevant works if the tenant had left voluntarily.

Reasonable prospects

When advising on 'reasonable prospects', you will need to consider the actual steps your client will need to take to put their plans into action. Available finance is frequently neglected but is easily cured as a matter of evidence.

In *Dolgellau Golf Club v Hett* (1998) 76 P&CR 526, the Court of Appeal held that a landlord had established his intention to re-occupy a remote golf course in Wales, notwithstanding that the project might lack financial viability. Auld LJ applied the observations of O'Connor LJ in *Cox v. Binfield* [1989] 1 EGLR 97 that the judge must be able to say objectively that the intention is one which is capable of being carried out in the reasonable future in the circumstances which will prevail when possession is achieved by the landlord. Auld LJ said at 534–5 that the test was one of intention and reasonable practicability:

> *...not of the probability of achieving its start or its likely success once established. It is not an incident of the statutory formula, nor of the present judicial gloss on it, that a landlord, in seeking to satisfy the court of the reality of his intention, should be subjected to minute examination of his finances with a view to determining the financial viability and durability of the business he intends to establish. The court is not there to police a landlord's entitlement to recover possession of his own property by examining the financial wisdom of his genuinely held plans for it. Nor will it always be appropriate to test the reasonable practicability of a landlord's intention to establish a business by*

> *reference to the presence or absence of detailed building plans, planning and licensing consents or indications and the like ...*

Notwithstanding these comments, it is important for a landlord to ensure that its plans can withstand sustained examination by the tenant and, if necessary, by the court.

One early, but useful, case as to the level of detail required to establish the ability to carry out the work is *Reohorn v Barry Corporation* [1956] 1 WLR 845. The tenant used the holding in question as a carpark. The landlord served a notice relying on ground (f). The landlord produced resolutions on a proposed comprehensive scheme for development of the land, and submitted an outline plan, which showed an extensive scheme, estimated to cost £500,000. They also produced a proposal to build a new road on the north of the site, which would improve the access to the shore and beaches on Barry Island, for which purpose expenditure of had been approved. They produced a letter from a development company with which they had been in correspondence stating that the company was agreed 'in principle' to start work on the scheme in June 1956, 'subject to the approval of the council and the conclusion of satisfactory arrangements.' They also produced evidence that it was proposed to form a new company which would take a building lease of the land. No one was called from the development company to give evidence before the county court as to the provision of the necessary finance or their financial stability. The corporation's engineer, surveyor and valuer gave evidence that the town planning authority had approved in general of the scheme, but that it could not proceed until vacant possession was obtained. The county court judge held that ground F had been established.

The Court of Appeal allowed the tenant's appeal. Denning LJ noted that no one from the development company had been called to give evidence; the financial stability and backing of the new company was unknown; there was only an outline plan and there would still have to be detailed negotiations about the plans, the nature of the buildings, the amount of rent, the terms of the lease, the timetable, etc. It was held at 849 that there were 'many difficulties still to be surmounted'. Although it was acceptable to use a building lease, here 'There is no building lease, no lessee in existence at the moment, no plans with any details, no knowledge of any financial backing.' (850). He cited Asquith LJ's words in *Cunliffe v Goodman* [1950] 2 KB 237, 254 that the matter was still in the region of 'the tentative, the provisional and the exploratory,' and had not yet reached 'the valley of decision.'

Planning permission

Frequently the most problematic issue is planning. It is not necessary to actually have planning permission. In *Cadogan v McCarthy & Stone (Developments) Ltd* [2000] L & TR 249, the Court of Appeal made it clear that the test to be applied was one of reasonable prospects, a real chance, of obtaining planning permission, a prospect sufficiently strong on the balance of probabilities to support a proposed course of action on which a reasonable landlord would embark. Savile LJ noted in *Cadogan*:

> *A reasonable prospect in this context accordingly means a real chance, a prospect that is strong enough to be acted on by a reasonable landlord minded to go ahead with plans which require permission, as opposed to a prospect that should be treated as merely fanciful or as one that should sensibly be ignored by a reasonable landlord. A reasonable prospect does not entail that it is more likely than not that permission will be obtained.*

The hurdle that the landlord has to surmount 'is by no means a high one': Laws LJ in *Gatwick Parking Services Ltd v Sargent* [2000] 2 EGLR 45. The assumption must be made that the landlord has recovered possession of the site and that the tenants had left before it made the planning application: *Westminster City Council v British Waterways Board* [1985] 1 AC 676.

It might occasionally be the case that the development does not require planning. If planning is a matter in issue, however, you should be prepared to support this. Sometimes, quite sophisticated points of planning law will need to be argued. You may also need to adduce expert evidence on the issue. This was the case in *Warwickshire Aviation Ltd v Littler Investments Ltd* [2019] EWHC 633 (Ch), where both parties called planning experts to opine as to the chances of successfully obtaining planning permission. Birss J agreed with the trial judge's view that the words 'reasonable prospect' speak for themselves, and that they are not susceptible to a statistical analysis.

In *Capocci v Goble* [1987] 2 EGLR 102, the landlord relied on ground F, arguing that she intended to develop a cold store and garage into 10 flats. She called the director of a building company who had previously carried out similar works. The tenant argued that substantial details of the proposed redevelopment remained to be worked out. The ultimate redevelopment would depend not only on the landlord's own volition, but also on, for instance, that of the developer or any alternative developer that may take its place. The Court of Appeal disagreed. The planning was clear and there was no obstacle to detailed planning permission. Although the financial aspect was not firm, the developer had done this sort of development in the same town before, the bank had confirmed its willingness and the architect had told them that there should be no obstacle to the development. It was not necessary to enter into a contract with the construction company; in fact, it was the developer who had approached the landlord.

Joint ventures with developers

Given the above discussion about the landlord's intention, it is appropriate to note that the landlord who intends to obtain vacant possession before selling the holding to a third party for development cannot rely on ground F (although, as noted above, they might be able to sell the land to the developer before the trial of the issue along with an assignment of the notice: it will then be for the developer to establish the ground).

In order to get around this, some landlords enter into a joint venture with a developer, sometimes through a building lease. In *Gilmour Caterers Ltd v St Bartholomew's Hospital Governors* [1956] 1 QB 387 the landlords opposed the grant of a new lease on the grounds that they intended to demolish and reconstruct the premises. They had made an agreement with a developer to grant a lease for a term of 48 years upon condition that he cleared the site and erected a new building. Denning LJ held that it was acceptable, for the purposes of ground F, to grant a building lease as a means of paying for the work. It is not necessary to show that the landlords must personally demolish or reconstruct and the agreement was just as effective as engaging building contractors. Subsequently, in *Spook Erection Ltd v British Railways Board* [1988] 1 EGLR 76, the building lease was to be for a term of 99 years. It was held that the landlord intended to do the work by a tenant/agent on his behalf under a building lease.

A more recent example of the structure of a joint venture is *Turner v Wandsworth London Borough Council* [1994] 1 EGLR 134. The holding in question was next to a private school owned by a limited company. The landlord entered into an agreement with the limited company whereby it would remove the hardstanding on the site, demolish the buildings on it and lay tarmac and landscape it; following this it would be granted a 4-year lease. Ultimately, the landlord wanted to sell the site when conditions were more favourable. The Court of Appeal held that the landlord's eventual motive for carrying out the works was irrelevant and a new tenancy was refused.

Time when the works will take place

The landlord will need to show that the works will start upon the termination of the tenancy. If the ground of opposition is made out, the tenancy will terminate three months after the claim is finally disposed of: section 64(1) LTA 1954. This 3-month period will start at the end of any appeal, or if no appeal is commenced, when the time limit to start an appeal has expired, which is normally 21 days from the date of the decision unless otherwise ordered: CPR 52.12(2).

In *Edwards v Thompson* (1990) 60 P & CR 222, the premises (a smithy) were part of a larger area of land. The landlord had planning permission but it required the construction of an access road before the new development could be occupied. The Court of Appeal held that although the landlord had shown that she had sufficient resources to develop the holding, it had to be considered as part of the overall development. On the evidence, Nourse LJ held that there was no reasonable prospect that on the termination of the tenancy she would herself be able to develop or a developer would be found: instead, 'It might well have been necessary to wait a matter of months'. The ground of opposition therefore failed. On the other hand, in *London Hilton Jewellers Ltd v Hilton International Ltd* [1990] 1 EGLR 112 the landlord was able to start work within a month or so of possession, and was able to succeed on this basis. See also *Method Developments v Jones* [1971] 1 WLR 168, a ground G case, where the landlord succeeded where they could move in 'within a reasonable time' of the termination of the tenancy.

Section 31(2) applies to ground F. This provides that where the landlord is unable to establish this ground or any other ground, but would be able to establish it at a later date (not more than a year later than the date specified) the court shall make a declaration to this effect and shall not make an order for the grant of a new tenancy. Instead, if within 14 days of the making of the declaration, the tenant can require the court to make an order substituting that new date for the date specified in the landlord's notice or tenant's request. This section is, however, rarely invoked.

Substantial work of construction

Ground F refers to a number of different construction scenarios within a few phrases. Breaking down the ground into its component parts it includes:

a) demolition of the premises comprised in the holding;

b) reconstruction of the premises comprised in the holding;

c) demolition of a substantial part of the premises comprised in the holding;

d) reconstruction of a substantial part of the premises comprised in the holding;

e) substantial work of construction on the holding;

f) substantial work of construction on part of the holding.

Each of these individual words have each attracted their own case law. You should be alert to ensure that you know which of these different elements your own case fits into. It might be that you can refer to a number of them.

Whether or not the works affect a 'substantial part' of the premises is a question of fact: *Atkinson v Bettison* [1955] 1 WLR 1127, where the decision of the trial judge against the landlord was upheld where only the ground floor shop front of a three storey building was to be altered. The emphasis is on the premises, rather than the occupation or use to which they are going to be put.

- 'Demolition' involves the physical act of destruction, and reconstruction is equivalent to rebuilding, and contemplates a state of affairs where there has been a measure of demolition falling short of total demolition;

- The word 'construction' involves work to build something that was not previously there: *Cook v Mott* (1961) 178 EG 637.

- The meaning of the word 'reconstruct' is best expressed by the synonym 'rebuild'. The word 'reconstruction' means a physical reconstruction of the premises. It involves a substantial interference with the structure of the premises and then a rebuilding, probably in a different form, of such part of the premises as has been demolished by reason of the interference with the structure.: *Percy E Cadle & Co Ltd v Jacmarch Properties Ltd* [1957] 1 QB 323;

- It is necessary to look at the whole of the work, and then decide as a matter of fact and common sense whether it amounts to demolition or reconstruction of a substantial part of the premises, or the carrying out of substantial work of construction on them: *Joel v Swaddle* [1957] 1 WLR 1094, 1099;

- Work associated with demolition and reconstruction, such as works of preparation ancillary to such works, or replastering and rewiring, or the laying of cables and drains, may be considered when looking at the totality of the work to determine whether the work is construction or is substantial or is on a substantial part of the premises: *Cerex Jewels Ltd v Peachey Property Corporation plc* [1986] 2 EGLR 65;

- For works to qualify as 'reconstruction' within ground F it must be shown that they are works of rebuilding involving a substantial interference with the structure of the building, but structure is not necessarily confined to outside or other load-bearing walls. Works of preparation ancillary to such works are properly included as works of reconstruction or construction. This also includes work closely associated with the completion of works of reconstruction: where a new load-bearing wall is being installed it would be right to include the plastering of that wall as an inseparable consequence of installation: *Romulus Trading Co Ltd v Henry Smith's Charity Trustees* [1990] 2 EGLR 75.

There are a number of reported cases, both at first instance and on appeal, where the landlord's plans for redevelopment have fallen either side of the threshold. To take two examples:

- 'Demolition': *Houseleys v Bloomer-Holt* [1966] 1 WLR 1244. The holding consisted of a small piece of land bounded on one side by a brick wall and having a garage covering about one-third of it. The landlords intended to demolish the garage and the wall and concrete the whole site to make an entry, exit and turning space for heavy lorries coming to and from their timber yard. It was held that a landlord can successfully oppose the grant of a new lease under the Landlord and Tenant Act 1954 on the ground in section 30(1)(f) that he intends to demolish the premises comprised in the holding if he shows an intention to demolish all the buildings on the holding, even though they cover only a minor part of it. The concreting of the whole of the holding was a 'substantial work of construction'.

- 'Reconstruction': *Ivorygrove Ltd v Global Grange Ltd* [2003] 1 WLR 2090. There was nothing in ground F which required the demolition or reconstruction of structural or load bearing features as a condition of its applicability. The landlord could show an intention to demolish and reconstruct a substantial part of the premises (namely most of the interior) and a substantial work of construction on the holding. It followed that the question of whether the relevant parts of the premises were load bearing was just one of the factors to be taken into consideration in the determination as to whether the works qualified as demolition or reconstruction within the meaning of ground F. It was a matter of fact and degree whether the replacement and reconfiguration of partition walls fell within ground F. This should be contrasted with the *dicta* of Stocker LJ in *Barth v Pritchard* [1990] 1 EGLR 109 at p111 that 'I would not consider wooden partitions, however extensive, as falling within the definition of 'construction', but such a situation would have to be reviewed in accordance with the facts of any given case.' The difference between the two cases was that in *Ivorygrove* (where *Barth* was cited) the partition walls were

> not the usual light weight demountable office partitions but were substantial, and that 'undoubted' structural works were also going to take place: again, this was a matter of fact and degree.

In some business leases, only the finishing surfaces, such as plaster on the walls, are demised: the structural elements are retained by the landlord. In such cases, ground F can be established by demolishing the parts that have been demised and incorporating the premises into a wider scheme of development: *Pumperninks of Piccadilly Ltd v Land Securities Plc* [2002] 2 EGLR 147 CA, where either (a) the premises actually demised would be demolished; or (b) as well as that demolition, the rights of support that rendered the demise capable of occupation would also be demolished. In the past, landlords have relied on the *Pumperninks* case to demonstrate that they reasonably require possession, even if the proposed modifications themselves were designed in such a way that they served no business purpose save for obtaining possession. It is likely that that the decision *Franses* will make it more difficult for a landlord to justify limited modifications designed solely to satisfy Ground F e.g. reducing or raising the height of the ceiling and / or floor, or moving walls.

The landlord will need to demonstrate that it has the right to carry out what could be disruptive or noisy works, especially if it has tenants in adjacent properties. In *London Kendal Street No3 Ltd v Daejan Investments Ltd* [2019] L. & T.R. 22, a decision of the County Court (Central London), the tenant argued that the landlord would be faced with an injunction preventing it from carrying out the intended works. This argument was rejected, however: it was held that any injunction (if granted) would not be absolute but would be tailored to protect the rights of both parties under the lease.

To establish that he or she requires possession a landlord will often need to call evidence from a professional advisor such as an architect or surveyor.

Landlord already possessing required powers of construction

The landlord must prove that it needs to terminate the tenancy to gain legal possession of the holding to carry out the works.

Occasionally, a covenant in the lease giving the landlord wide ranging powers of entry to do works will be fatal to establishing ground F. This is because there is no need for the landlord to recover possession in order to carry out the works: instead, it can simply proceed under its extensive powers under the lease.

In *Heath v Drown* [1973] AC 498 the tenant's lease reserved to the landlord, '*the right at all reasonable hours upon notice to enter upon the demised premises . . . for the purpose of carrying out necessary repairs.*' The landlord opposed the renewal of the tenancy under the Landlord and Tenant Act 1954 on the ground that he intended to carry out substantial reconstruction of the building and could not reasonably do so without obtaining possession of the tenant's two floors for several months. The House of Lords noted that what the landlord proposed to do was not demolition, which would have caused the holding to cease to exist physically, nor was it properly described as reconstruction of the premises, since at the end of the operation the premises would exist exactly as they existed before, with the holdings now occupied by the tenant continuing to be capable of being leased out of the premises. They were instead 'substantial work of construction'. It was held that where the landlord can enter and do the works under the terms of the lease it is not necessary to terminate it to enable the landlord to do the work. In that case, the tenant was entitled to a new lease.

Obligation to grant new tenancy where development can be carried out

Section 31A is a detailed provision that parallels the situation where a landlord already has sufficient powers under the lease to carry out the proposed works of development. Under section 31A, a tenant can either:

a) (section 31A(1)(a)) agree that the new lease it will be granted will include terms giving the landlord access and 'other facilities' to carry out the work intended (section 31A(1)(a)). Here, the provision emphasises that it applies where landlord can:

    a. 'reasonably carry out the work without obtaining possession of the holding' and

   b. 'without interfering to a substantial extent or for a substantial time with the use of the holding for the purpose of the business carried on by the tenant'; or

b) (section 31A(1)(b)) agree to accept a tenancy of an economically separable part of the holding and either

   a. is willing to accept further terms in the lease of the part that he retains, as per section 31A(1)(a); or

   b. possession of the remainder of the holding would be reasonably sufficient to enable the landlord to carry out the intended work.

The works in section 31A(1) are the works of demolition, reconstruction or construction referred to in section 30(1)(f).

A part of a holding is an 'economically separable part' in section 31A(1)(b) by reference to the rent payable. Section 31A(2) states that it falls within this definition '*if, and only if, the aggregate of the rents which, after the completion of the intended work, would be reasonably obtainable on separate lettings of that part and the remainder of the premises affected by or resulting from the work would not be substantially less than the rent which would then be reasonably obtainable on a letting of those premises as a whole.*'

In considering this provision, the court must start with the works which the landlord actually intends to carry out; for the court has no power to curtail the landlord's scheme of works, or to inquire into his actual needs: *Decca Navigator Co. v Greater London Council* [1974] 1 WLR 748.

A landlord will be able to defeat a tenant's argument under section 31A if there is interference with a tenant's actual use of the holding to a substantial extent or for a substantial time. The reference to 'substantial interference' relates to the physical use of the premises, as opposed to the effect of the work on the tenant's business: *Redfern v Reeves* (1978) 37 P & CR 364, where a tenant's argument that she could move out for one or two months during the works did not prevent her tenancy from being terminated. This is, again, a question of fact: see *Blackburn v Hussain* [1988] 1 EGLR 77 CA, where a period of eight weeks was not enough to engage ground F.

Change of circumstances before appeal

It is not unusual for the factual matrix to change following the final decision but before an appeal. For example, a refused planning application could be overturned on appeal to the Planning Inspector. There is a line of case law that makes it clear that the appellate court is entitled to take this change of circumstances into account. In *Gatwick Parking Services Ltd v Sargent* [2000] 2 EGLR 45, Laws LJ stated that he was 'entirely clear that we are now entitled to take account of [subsequent] planning permission' that followed the trial at first instance, citing *Accountancy Personnel Ltd v Salters' Company* [1972] EGD 461. Lewison J (as he then was) explained the rationale for this approach in *Davy's of London (Wine Merchants) Ltd v City of London Corp* [2004] EWHC 2224 (Ch) at [48]: 'Unlike the position in most civil cases, the judge in an application for a new tenancy is not deciding what happened in the past, but what terms should govern the future. This, perhaps, explains why the court is more ready to admit evidence of post-trial events in such cases. The point is all the stronger in a case in which, as here, the dispute turns on an evaluation of future events.' This explanation of the rationale for the approach in the *Davy's* case was confirmed in *Clear Call Ltd v Central London Investments Ltd* [2016] EWCA Civ 1231, [2017] L & TR 13, where the tenant's application to adduce further evidence about a comparable letting in a rent determination case was refused, as the evidence was in respect of past, not future, events: the tenant's application also failed the test in *Ladd v Marshall* [1954] 1 WLR 1489 for fresh evidence on appeal.

CHECKLIST – making out ground F

- Ensure that it was the relevant landlord who served the notice and who can establish ground F.

- Make sure that the landlord can prove ground F on the termination of the relevant termination. This is calculated as 21 days from the date of the hearing, plus 3 months.

- The landlord must subjectively intend to carry out the works.

- The landlord's intent to carry out the works must be independent of whether or not the tenant moves out voluntarily i.e. it cannot simply be a means to the end of obtaining possession: see *Franses*

- The landlord must have 'reasonable prospects' of being able to carry out the works. This can include:

  - Planning;

  - Finance;

  - Contractors / developers.

- The works must include:

  - Demolition or reconstruction of the premises in the holding;

  - Demolition or reconstruction of a substantial part of those premises;

  - Substantial works of construction on the holding;

  - Substantial work of construction on part of the holding.

- The landlord must show that it cannot carry out these works without obtaining possession. Check the repair clauses in your lease to make sure that they are not so wide that the landlord does not need to terminate the lease.

- Consider section 31A: if the tenant's new lease contained appropriate covenants allowing the landlord access, could the landlord reasonably carry out the work?

CHAPTER EIGHTEEN

GROUND G – LANDLORD INTENDS TO OCCUPY THE HOLDING

> *(g) subject as hereinafter provided, that on the termination of the current tenancy the* ***landlord intends to occupy the holding for the purposes****, or partly for the purposes, of a* **business** *to be carried on by him therein, or as his* ***residence***

Under ground G, a landlord can recover possession of the holding for the purposes, or at least partly for the purposes, of their own business or residence. Ground G appears deceptively simple: after all, most landlords want to recover possession for their 'own use', including re-letting. Ground G does not allow for the recovery of possession simply for re-letting: instead, the landlord must establish that it will itself occupy the holding for a business that it carries on itself. This ground is limited by other statutory provisions. It is also necessary to satisfy the same test of intention that was explored in the previous chapter.

Eligibility to rely on ground (g)

Section 30(2) LTA 1954 introduces lengthy eligibility criteria based on the length of time that the landlord has owned its interest as the landlord:

> *(2) The landlord shall not be entitled to oppose an application under section 24(1) of this Act, or make an application under section 29(2) of this Act, on the ground specified in paragraph (g) of the last foregoing subsection if the interest of the landlord, or an interest which has merged in that interest and but for the merger would be the interest of the landlord, was purchased or created after the beginning of the period of five years which ends with the termination of the current tenancy, and at all times since the purchase or creation thereof the holding has been comprised in a tenancy or successive tenancies of the description specified in subsection (1) of section twenty-three of this Act.*

It is this provision (the so-called 'five year rule') often catches out and prevents landlords from relying on ground G as it stops a new purchaser from relying on this ground.

This does not, however, prevent a landlord from transferring its interest to a successor in title for no consideration, as the word 'purchased' in the section has its popular meaning 'bought for money: *HL Bolton Engineering Co Ltd v TJ Graham & Co Ltd* [1957] 1 QB 159. In that case, the merger of interests by surrender of an intermediate lease, did not amount to a "purchase" by the superior landlord so as to debar it from relying upon ground G.

Companies

Section 30(1)(1A) was introduced to clarify the situation where a landlord intends to run a business through a company. It confirms that the reference in ground G to 'the landlord' will include a reference to the landlord or its company where it has a controlling stake in that company.

Where the landlord is a company and a person has a controlling interest in that company, section 30(1B) confirms that the reference in ground G to 'the landlord' shall be construed as a reference to either the company or that person. This provision has its own five-year eligibility rule, however: section 30(2A) states that (1B) does not apply if:

a) the controlling interest was acquired after the beginning of the period of five years which ends with the termination of the current tenancy; and

b) at all times since the acquisition of the controlling interest the holding has been comprised in a tenancy or successive tenancies of the description specified in section 23(1) of the LTA 1954 (*i.e.* 'property comprised in the tenancy is or includes premises which are occupied by the tenant and are so occupied for the purposes of a business carried on by him or for those and other purposes': see Chapter 2).

Section 42(3) deals with the situation where the landlord's interest is held by a member of a group of companies. In these circumstances, the reference to 'intended occupation by the landlord for the purposes of a business to be carried on by him' includes intended occupation by any member of the group for the purposes of a business to be carried on by that member: section 42(3)(a). Further, the reference in section 30(2) to the purchase or creation of any interest 'shall be construed as a reference to a purchase from or creation by a person other than a member of the group': section 42(3)(b) (author's emphasis).

Trusts

Section 41(2) states that where the landlord's interest is held on trust, references in ground G to the landlord also include references to the beneficiaries under the trust, or any of them. The reference in section 30(2) (the five-year rule) to the 'creation of the interest' will therefore include the creation of the trust.

There are limitations to this provision. In *Frish Ltd v Barclays Bank Ltd* [1955] 2 QB 541, the Court of Appeal decided that there must indeed be a limitation upon the wide words 'beneficiaries, or any of them' in section 41(2). Sir Raymond Evershed MR held that only those beneficiaries whose interest under the trust is such as to give them the right, as against the trustees, to occupy the property, or is such that the trustees may properly within the terms of their trust let them as beneficiaries into possession, can rely on this provision. If the intended occupation is to be that of a beneficiary, it must be shown that it is the intention that he should so occupy by virtue of his quality or right as a beneficiary. In *Frish* the proposed occupier was a beneficiary under a discretionary trust: this was not enough to bring them within ground G.

This rule has been understood to mean that in the case of a public charitable trust there are no beneficiaries whose occupation or intended occupation may be relied on. In *Parkes v Westminster Roman Catholic Diocese Trustee* (1978) 36 P & CR 22, the Westminster Roman Catholic Diocese Trustee could not rely on section 41(2) and had to argue that it was carrying on the 'business' itself. In that case, it was held that they could rely on the activities of a priest, Father Barry, to be occupation (as agent) on the Trustee's behalf.

In *Meyer v Riddick* (1990) 60 P & CR 50 it was held that if a beneficiary under a trust is to rely section 41(2), he or she must establish that he is entitled to occupy the property by virtue of his or her interest under the trust. In order to get around *Frish*, the three trustees for sale of land proposed to grant a lease to two of themselves. As these two were going to occupy under a lease and not because of their status as beneficiaries they could not rely on section 41(2).

On the other hand, occupation by the trustees themselves is within section 41(2), even if the trust was created within the five year period: *Morar v Chauhan* [1985] 3 All ER 493. In that case the freeholder, C, transferred premises to trustees which they held on trust for C. The trustees demised the premises to tenants. The trustees subsequently transferred the premises back to C, who executed a declaration of trust of the premises in favour of his children. C gave the tenants section 25 Notices, relying on, amongst others, ground G. May LJ held that where the landlord of business premises is a trustee for one or more beneficiaries, then the subsection *prima facie* entitles those beneficiaries as well as the landlord to oppose the grant of a new tenancy relying on ground G. The second part of s 41(2) places such beneficiaries under a similar 'limitation' as there would be on the landlord were he alone beneficially entitled to the reversion: if the trust under which the beneficiaries acquired their beneficial interest was created within the preceding five years, then they too are barred from relying on ground G.

Partnerships

There is no express provision for 'landlord' partnerships under the LTA 1954 as there is for companies or as in the case of 'tenant' partnerships for the purpose of service of notices (section 41A).

In the case of *Re Crowhurst Park* [1974] 1 WLR 583, the landlord relied on ground G on the basis that he intended to carry on a business in partnership with his wife. This was held to fall within this ground. Goulding J noted, at 589, that 'Where two persons carry on business in common as partners each of them occupies the firm's premises and each of them carries on business.' The landlord may also seek to rely upon the trust provisions of the LTA 1954, discussed above.

Intention

The test of intention is the same as that as for ground F. Reference should be made to the section in Chapter 17.

In particular, a landlord will need to establish, following the *S Franses Ltd v Cavendish Hotel (London) Ltd* [2018] UKSC 62 case, that it would intend to occupy the holding itself whether or not the tenant moved out voluntarily. In the past, some landlords advanced proposals which were devised only to satisfy ground G. Following *Franses*, it is likely that courts will examine the quality of the landlord's intent to occupy to ensure that it is not 'conditional' on the recovery of possession.

It was already the case that a landlord would expect to have the genuineness of its motivation examined closely in a ground G case. In the first instance decision in *Patel v Ramraj* (Oxford County Court) [2018] 7 WLUK 150, it was accepted that the credibility of the landlord was a key issue in arriving at a subjective assessment of the state of mind of the landlord as at the date of the hearing, following *Zarvos v Pradhan* [2003] EWCA Civ 208; [2003] 2 P&CR 9. Ward LJ stated in the Court of Appeal at [22] in respect of the first, subjective, limb of intent that if the "*expression of that intent [by the landlord] was a colourable device to obtain possession and then do something different with the premises, that is the end of the matter.*"

A landlord does not have to intend to occupy the premises personally: it can satisfy ground G by intending to occupy and carry on his business through an agent, manager or sub-contractor: *Hills (Patents) Ltd. v University College Hospital Board of Governors* [1956] 1 QB 90, *Parkes v Westminster Roman Catholic Diocese Trustee* (1978) 36 P & CR 22.

In *Hills (Patents) Ltd*, Denning LJ drew a distinction between possession, which in law is single and exclusive, and occupation. The latter may be shared with others or had on behalf of others. Where a board of governors intended to sell a hospital to the Minister for Health, but to continue to run it themselves as a hospital, it was held that they were entitled to succeed on the basis that they would be the occupiers. It was doubtful, however, if the owner of a shop who wanted to sell it to a chain store while he would continue to manage it could satisfy ground G as he would not be occupying it for the purpose of his business.

It is possible for a landlord to attempt to fortify his claim that he or she holds the requisite intent by giving an undertaking to the court to use the premises themselves. The court may give such weight to an undertaking in these circumstances as is appropriate: see, for example, *Lennox v Bell*

(1957) 169 EG 753. The court is not, however, bound in any way by such an undertaking. In *Patel v Keles* [2010] Ch 332 the limited nature of the landlord's offer of an undertaking appeared to undermine rather than bolster his case. In the appropriate case, such an undertaking can prove decisive: in *London Hilton Jewellers Ltd v Hilton International Hotels Ltd* [1990] 1 EGLR 112 it was held that it showed fixity of intention following a review of the relevant authorities.

The question of the landlord's intentions is a question of fact. In *Herbert v Blakey (Bradford)* Ltd (1956) 167 EG 65 the landlords had been ready to sell the premises to the tenant for several years and had offered to do so, leading him to believe that they did not the premises for their own purposes. Denning LJ held that the burden was on the landlords to prove they had a firm and settled intention to use the premises for their own business purposes. Whether the court was satisfied they had such an intention was a matter for the first instance judge. The landlord's appeal was rejected.

A recent and useful illustration of establishing intention under ground G was *Humber Oil Terminals Trustee Ltd v Associated British Ports* [2011] L & TR 27. In that case the Judge considered the two limbs of the intention test together as the question of what was likely to happen at the end of the lease and whether the landlord could, in practice, occupy the premises for its own purposes turned on what third parties decided to do. This meant that it was more appropriate to consider the statutory test holistically. Although there would be difficulties for the landlord to carry out the project, it was what it did intend to do.

The landlord might face some difficulty establishing the requisite intention if it only intends to occupy the holding in the short term. In *Willis v Association of Universities of the British Commonwealth* [1965] 1 QB 140 the landlord company intended to occupy the premises for the purposes of its business, but had passed a resolution to enter liquidation for the purposes of reconstruction and to transfer its assets to a successor company in order to convert from a limited company into a chartered company. The landlord would, therefore, only be in occupation for a short period. Lord Denning MR noted that 'Section 30(1)(g) of the 1954 Act does not say for how long the landlord must intend to occupy himself, and the courts must fill the gap.' He went on to comment that just as a purchaser within the previous five years cannot defeat the tenant (see section 30(2)), so also a purchaser shortly afterwards should not be able to defeat him. On the facts, where the landlord did intend to occupy and then to transfer their activities to a successor for no payment or anything in the nature of a sale (so that, to Pearson LJ, the landlord and the successor company were in substance one and the same), the landlords satisfied the ground of opposition. It was stated, however, that an intention to sell in a short period after possession was recovered would mean that the landlord had not shown the necessary intention. This followed an analogy with section 30(2) and the 'five-year rule', discussed above.

In *Patel v Keles* [2010] Ch 332, the judge at first instance held that although the landlords had no settled intention to sell the premises, they were highly likely to sell them after two years and, in the circumstances, lacked the intention required by section 30(1)(g). The Court of Appeal dismissed the landlords' appeal. Arden LJ noted the analogy made with the 'five-year rule' drawn in *Willis*, commenting that section 30(2) was 'an indication that Parliament cannot have intended section 30(1)(g) to be available to a landlord if he had already formed the intention to sell at the date of the application or hearing because that would be a way of driving a coach and horses through the protection given by section 30(2)'.

Carrying on a business as a partnership is enough for ground G: *Re Crowhurst Park* [1974] 1 WLR 583. In *Jones v Jenkins* [1986] 1 EGLR 113 the landlord intended to let out the holding for residential accommodation: as she did not intend to occupy them, it fell outside ground G, applying *Bagettes Ltd v G.P. Estates Ltd* [1956] Ch 290.

Landlord's own business

The landlord must intend to occupy the premises 'within a reasonable time' from the date of the termination of the current tenancy. In *Method Developments v Jones* [1971] 1 WLR 168 the landlord only required a proportion of the holding for immediate use; the rest was not immediately required but would be taken into use in the near future when additional staff would have to be accommodated. It was held that there was a settled intention to use a very substantial part of the premises in question immediately, and everything except 400 square feet within a short time. Salmon LJ held that 'paragraph (g) must cover a situation such as the present where the landlords intend at the termination of the lease – which must mean within a reasonable time from the date of its termination – to enter into occupation of all the holding and use a part of it for the purposes of their business.' He added at 173 that 'just as you can plainly occupy a dwelling-house as your residence even though you leave a couple of rooms empty, I think here that these landlords proved an intention to occupy the whole of this holding for the purposes of their business.'

It is not necessary, however, for the landlord to prove that he or she will physically occupy the premises themselves without help from others. In *Skeet and another v Powell-Sheddon* [1988] 2 EGLR 112 the landlord gave evidence that she would enter into a partnership agreement with her husband, who would be responsible for the day-to-day management of the hotel, while her daughter would finish her studies in hotel management and move in as manageress. The landlord would not move in herself. Russell LJ held that was no need for her to demonstrate that she counted on carrying on the business exclusively.

Residence

Ground G also includes the possibility that the landlord intends to occupy the premises 'as his residence'. In practice, this possibility is rarely seen. It is likely to be a question of fact and degree whether a landlord intends to occupy the premises as his or her residence, especially where the landlord does not intend to make the premises their only home.

Alterations

In *Nursey v Currie (P) (Dartford) Ltd* [1959] 1 WLR 273, the Court of Appeal stated that the 'holding' was the building let to the tenant. In that case, the landlords wanted to demolish the building and develop the site. As a consequence, it was held that the landlords had failed to show that they intended to occupy that holding for a business to be carried on by them.

Despite this decision, there have been successful applications under this ground when the landlord intended to alter the premises, *Cam Gears v Cunningham* [1981] 1 WLR 1011 and *Method Developments v Jones* [1971] 1 WLR 168 being examples. It was also doubted in *Leathwoods*

Ltd v Total Oil Great Britain Ltd [1985] 2 EGLR 237, where Oliver LJ referred to the conflicting cases (including the decision of the Privy Council in *McKenna v Porter Motors Ltd* [1956] AC 688), stating that *Nursey's case* 'is a decision which is confined very much to the peculiar facts of that case'.

Although *Nursey's case* has never been formally overruled, it is unlikely that a properly directed court would follow its surprising outcome in the face of such trenchant commentary.

Effect of finding that ground G has been made out

Ground G is a mandatory and not a discretionary ground: once it has been established the court must refuse to grant a new tenancy to the tenant: *Skeet and another v Powell-Sheddon* [1988] 2 EGLR 112.

CHAPTER NINETEEN
COMPENSATION FOR NO-FAULT TERMINATION

Introduction

The LTA 1954 provides for compensation in certain circumstances for tenants who do not obtain a new tenancy as a result of the landlord's reliance on Grounds E, F and/or G. The applicability of those grounds is dealt with in chapters 16, 17 and 18. A unifying feature of the three compensation grounds is that they arise in circumstances where the tenant is deprived of a new tenancy through no fault of its own.

There are other instances where some form of compensation may become payable in respect of premises used for business purposes. For example, section 37(A) of LTA 1954 deals with compensation payable as a result of possession having been obtained by the landlord by misrepresentation; we deal with that provision in chapter 11. Subject to compliance with strict procedures under the Landlord and Tenant Act 1927, compensation may also be payable in certain circumstances for improvements carried out by the tenant; we deal with that legislation in chapter 22.

What is a compensation ground?

Section 37(1A) of LTA 1954 defines Grounds E (uneconomic sub-letting), F (reconstruction/redevelopment) and G (intended landlord occupation) as 'the compensation grounds'.

What is a compensation case?

Procedurally, section 37 (1) LTA 1954 introduces three scenarios where, on quitting the holding, the tenant shall be entitled to compensation from the landlord. These scenarios are set out in sub-sections (1A) to (1C) and are termed 'compensation cases'.

The first compensation case arises where the tenant brings a claim for a new tenancy pursuant to section 24(1) LTA 1954 and the court is precluded from making an order for the grant of a new tenancy on any of the compensation grounds but not as a result of any other ground, see section 37(1A) LTA 1954.

So, this deals with the standard scenario where the landlord serves a Section 25 Notice (or the tenant makes a Section 26 Request), the tenant goes on to make a claim for a new tenancy and that claim fails as a result of the landlord establishing one of the compensation grounds. Note that if the landlord also succeeds in opposing the grant of a new tenancy on any other ground the tenant will *not* be entitled to compensation.

The second scenario arises where the landlord applies to terminate the tenancy pursuant to section 29(2) LTA 1954 and the court is precluded from granting the tenant a new tenancy as a result of one of the three compensation grounds; again, if a non-compensation ground is made out in addition, no compensation is payable.

The third scenario arises if the landlord has specified any of the compensation grounds and no other ground in its Section 25 Notice (or section 26(6) counter-notice to a tenant's Section 26 Request). In this scenario, if the tenant does not then apply under section 24(1) for a new tenancy, and the landlord does not apply to terminate the tenancy, then the tenant is entitled to compensation on quitting the holding. Similarly, if the tenant makes an application for a new tenancy but subsequently withdraws the claim the tenant will be entitled to compensation on quitting the holding.

To be entitled to compensation the tenant must, additionally, in each case 'quit the holding'.

If the case progresses to court and the court is precluded from ordering a new tenancy on compensation grounds only (*i.e.* in scenarios 1 or 2 above) the court is required, on the application of the tenant, to certify that fact: see section 37(4) LTA 1954.

How much?

Broadly speaking (subject to caveats regarding domestic property), the amount of compensation is calculated by reference to a multiple of the rateable value of the holding: see section 37(2) of the Act. 'The holding', as we have seen, means the property comprised in the tenancy less any part thereof which is neither occupied by the tenant nor by any person employed for the purposes of the business, section 23(3) LTA 1954.

Provision is made for the Secretary of State to set an "appropriate multiplier". Since the 1st April 1990 that multiplier has been 1, see the Landlord and Tenant Act 1954 (Appropriate Multiplier) Order 1990 (S.I. 1990/363).

The basic level of compensation is the rateable value of the holding multiplied by the appropriate multiplier; given, and whilst, the multiplier is 1 it can currently be left out of account.

If certain conditions set out in section 37(3) of the Act are met, then the tenant is entitled to double the compensation that would otherwise be payable.

The conditions are:

a) that during the whole of the period of 14 years immediately preceding the termination of the current tenancy, premises bring or comprised in the holding have been occupied for the purposes of a business carried on by the occupier or for those and other purposes;

b) that if, during those 14 years there was a change of occupier of the premises, the person who was the occupier immediately after the change was the successor to the business carried on by the person who was the occupier immediately before the change.

To work out the 14-year period, one needs to know the 'date of termination of the current tenancy'. For the purpose of the compensation provisions, this is taken to be the date specified as the date of termination in the section 25 Notice or Section 26 Request, section 37(7) LTA 1954.

As a result of changes effected by the 2003 Order, the Act now provides a more sophisticated approach to the situation where parts of the holding have been occupied for 14 years or more whereas others have not. The position now is that the differing parts of the holding are treated separately so that double compensation can apply for one part or parts of the holding whereas single compensation applies for other parts. The tenant is then entitled to the aggregate compensation by adding the separate sums together, see section 37(3A) LTA 1954.

It will be apparent from the above discussion that it can be important to ascertain how long the holding, and its various parts, have been occupied for business purposes. If taking an assignment of the term it would therefore be worth giving consideration to obtaining evidence at that time, whilst the assignee is engaged, incentivised and co-operative, as to its length of continuous business occupation so that it can be used if necessary at a later stage.

It is important to appreciate that the period required for double compensation is continuous and that one runs back from the specified termination date in the relevant notice. The court would appear to take a realistic view, however, as to whether the tenant has remained in continuous occupation. So, if there is a good business reason for a period of absence (say, as a result of damage to the property) that may not constitute a break in occupation for these purposes.

That said, it is best not to court controversy and argument if possible and the tenant would be well advised, particularly towards the end of the relationship where the landlord's antennae might well be engaged, to maintain an overt presence at the property. A case that pushes the boundaries in this area is *Bacchiocchi v Academic Ltd* [1998] 1 WLR 1313 where the tenant had returned the keys to the premises 12 days or so prior to the date specified in the notice as part of its plans to vacate. The Court of Appeal took a somewhat lenient view that this period did not constitute cessation of occupation (in a case in fact on the similarly worded provisions in section 38 LTA 1954 regarding contracting out of the compensation provisions). Contrast *Sight and Sound Education Ltd v Books Etc Ltd* [1999] 3 EGLR 45 where the tenant had gone out of occupation at or around the contractual term date, 5 months prior to the termination date in the Section 25 Notice, and double compensation was denied.

The rateable value for the holding is taken as at the date the landlord serves the Section 25 Notice or the tenant serves its Section 26 Request, as the case maybe, see section 37(5) LTA 1954. The sub-section goes on to make provision for the scenarios where part only of the holding is listed and where the rateable value cannot be ascertained by reference to the list; provision is also made for any dispute as to the rateable value of the holding to be referred to the Commissioners of Inland Revenue for decision by a valuation officer (with an appeal to lie to the Upper Tribunal).

What if there is domestic property within the holding? (We assume here that any cases the reader will be dealing with will concern valuation date post 1st April 1990 – different provisions apply otherwise). The LTA 1954 provides that if *the entirety* of the holding is domestic property (as defined in section 66 of the Local Government Finance Act 1988), then the rateable value shall be taken to be an amount equal to the rent at which the holding might reasonably be expected to be let on a tenancy from year if the tenant undertook to pay all usual tenant rates and taxes and to bear the cost of repairs, insurance and other expenses necessary to maintain the holding in a state to command that rent.

If *part only* of the holding is 'domestic property' within the meaning of section 66 of the Local Government Finance Act, then section 37(5A) LTA 1954 provides that the domestic part be disregarded and one calculates the rateable value of the holding to ascertain the compensation (or double compensation) attributable to the remainder of the holding. However, if, on the date of service of the Section 25 Notice or the Section 26 Request, the tenant occupied the whole or any part of the domestic property he is entitled to have added to his compensation "*a sum equal to his reasonable expenses in removing from the domestic property*". That sum is to be arrived at by agreement, failing which by determination of the court – see section 37(5B) LTA 1954.

Lastly, in the case of a severed reversion of various parts of the holding, section 37(3B) LTA 1954 provides that the claim for compensation lies in relation to each part against the person who satisfies the landlord conditions set out in section 44 in respect of that part.

Contracting out

Can the parties contract out of the compensation provisions? Yes, providing section 38(2) of the LTA 1954 does not apply.

Section 38(2) LTA 1954 contains provisions which restrict the parties' ability to exclude or reduce compensation payable under section 37.

Section 38(2) applies where during the whole of the 5 years immediately before the date on which the tenant is to quit the holding premises being or comprised in the holding have been occupied for the purposes of a business carried on by the occupier, or for those and other purposes. If, during those 5 years, there has been a change in occupier and the new occupier succeeds to the business of the predecessor, the predecessor's period of occupation can be used to make up the requisite 5 year period, see section 38(2)(b).

Where section 38(2) applies, any agreement which '*purports to exclude or reduce compensation under section 37*' is void to that extent. A limited exception, however, is made in favour of an agreement '*as to the amount*' of compensation providing that agreement is made '*after the right to compensation has accrued*'. The Act is not particularly clear as to precisely when the right to compensation accrues but the statutory language of section 37(1) LTA 1954 suggests it is the date the tenant '*quits the holding*'.

CHAPTER TWENTY

INTERIM CONTINUATION AND INTERIM RENT

Interim continuation

As noted above in chapters 10 and 8 respectively, where a landlord serves a section 25 Notice or where a tenant serves a section 26 Notice, the tenancy will expire on the date given in the notice unless an application is made to court.

Once an application is made, until such time as the new tenancy is granted or the application is disposed of, the tenancy will not be terminated (section 64(1) LTA 1954). The tenancy therefore continues in the interim.

Interim continuation after end of application to the court

The unsuccessful end of a tenant's application to the court for a new tenancy, or the successful conclusion of a landlord's opposition to a new tenancy in court proceedings, does not immediately terminate the tenancy. Instead, there is a 'sunset' interim continuation of the tenancy for a further three months under section 64(1) LTA 1954. This three months starts on the earliest date by which the proceedings on the application (including any proceedings on or in consequence of an appeal) have been determined and any time for appealing or further appealing has expired, except that if the application is withdrawn or any appeal is abandoned the reference shall be construed as a reference to the date of the withdrawal or abandonment.

For example, if on a trial on the preliminary issue as to whether the landlord makes out a ground of opposition under section 30(1) the landlord is successful, the three-month period will start 21 days after the date of the decision as this is the date when the time limit for lodging an appeal expires: CPR, r52.12(2)(b). If an appeal is lodged in this time, the tenancy will again continue in the interim. If the appeal is discontinued, the three-month time limit will start from the date when the appeal came to an end. If the appeal is unsuccessful, the tenancy will end 21 days plus three months later.

You should be aware that if the landlord applies to the court for the grant of a new tenancy to the tenant, but then the tenant informs the court that they do not want a new tenancy so that the application is dismissed (see section 29(5) LTA 1954: 'The court shall dismiss an application by the landlord under section 24(1) of this Act if the tenant informs the court that he does not want a new tenancy'), the tenant will have to pay the landlord's costs. This was the result of the case in *Lay v Drexler* [2007] 2 EGLR 46. The Court of Appeal explained that the purpose of this provision was to give a right to landlords to commence proceedings so that, by those proceedings, or the threat of them, landlords could compel tenants to make clear at an early stage their intentions as to whether they were seeking the grant of a new tenancy and, thereafter, to pursue negotiations to arrive at agreed terms for the grant of such a new tenancy. When the tenants filed an acknowledgement of service to the claim, they committed themselves to proceedings where they might have to pay costs.

Interim rent

When an application for a new tenancy is made and the statutory continuation applies, the tenant will continue to pay rent at the existing rate. This can lead to unfairness if the rental market has changed significantly since that rent was set.

The Law of Property Act 1969 introduced the idea of an 'interim rent' that would be payable from when the renewal process began until the new tenancy was granted or the existing one was terminated. This process was again amended by the RRO. The principle change made was that either the landlord or the tenant can apply for interim rent.

If a landlord has given a section 25 Notice or the tenant has applied under section 26 for a new tenancy, then either the landlord or the tenant can apply to the court to determine an 'interim rent': section 24A(1). It is not possible for a party to apply if the other has already made such an application and not withdrawn it: section 24A(2).

The interim rent is the rent that the tenant will pay while the tenancy continues under section 24.

The application must be made within six months of the termination of the relevant tenancy: section 24A(3).

When the amount payable as interim rent becomes payable

The interim rent determined on an application under section 24A is payable from the 'appropriate date'. This is defined, in section 24B, as either:

- in a case where the landlord has given a notice under section 25, the earliest date of termination that could have been specified in the landlord's notice (section 24B(2)); or
- in a case where the tenant has made a request for a new tenancy under section 26, the earliest date that could have been specified in the tenant's request as the date from which the new tenancy is to begin (section 24B(3)).

The amount payable as interim rent is therefore backdated. It can be a very useful tool for the landlord to put pressure on the tenant where the rent currently being paid is much lower than the market rent.

Amount of interim rent

The amount of interim rent payable is governed by sections 24C and 24D.

Non-opposed grant of tenancy where (a) interim rent will not differ substantially from the rent under the new tenancy or (b) the terms of the new tenancy will be substantially the same

Section 24C applies where:

- either the landlord has served a section 25 notice not opposing the grant of a new tenancy, or has not served a section 26(6) notice in response to a tenant's section 26 notice (i.e. the grant of a new tenancy is not opposed by the landlord); and

- the landlord grants a new tenancy of the whole of the property comprised in the relevant tenancy to the tenant.

In these circumstances, the interim rent will also be the rent payable under the new tenancy: section 24C(2). There are two exceptions to section 24C(2):

- the landlord or the tenant shows to the satisfaction of the court that the interim rent under that subsection differs substantially from the relevant rent (that is, the rent which (in default of agreement between the landlord and the tenant) the court would have determined under section 34 of this Act to be payable under the new tenancy if the new tenancy had commenced on the appropriate date). This exception therefore depends on the extent to which the market has moved; or

- the landlord or the tenant shows to the satisfaction of the court that the terms of the new tenancy differ from the terms of the relevant tenancy to such an extent that the interim rent under that subsection is substantially different from the rent which (in default of such agreement) the court would have determined under section 34 to be payable under a tenancy which commenced on the same day as the new tenancy and whose other terms were the same as the relevant tenancy. This exception therefore depends on the extent to which the terms of the lease have changed.

Opposition to grant of a tenancy, or (a) the rent payable under the new tenancy will be substantially different to the interim rent, or (b) the terms of the new tenancy will be substantially different

Section 24D applies in cases where section 24C does not apply (for example, where the new tenancy is opposed by the landlord, or where the new tenancy will not be the whole of the property in the relevant tenancy). Section 24D(1) defines the interim rent as 'the rent which it is reasonable for the tenant to pay while the relevant tenancy continues by virtue of section 24 of this Act.' When deciding this, subsections (1) and (2) of section 34 shall apply to the determination as they would apply to the determination of a rent under that section if a new tenancy from year to year of the whole of the property comprised in the relevant tenancy were granted to the tenant by order of the court. The court will also have regard to:

- to the rent payable under the terms of the relevant tenancy; and
- the rent payable under any sub-tenancy of part of the property comprised in the relevant tenancy.

No need for further application in certain circumstances

If the court has made a determination under section 24C, but either (a) the court subsequently revokes under section 36(2) of this Act the order for the grant of a new tenancy, or (b) the landlord and tenant agree not to act on the order, then the court on the application of the landlord or the tenant shall determine a new interim rent in accordance with subsections (1) and (2) above without a further application under section 24A(1).

Considerations to take into account

- Not all parties remember to apply for interim rent, even if it would be to their advantage. There can be a number of reasons for this. A party may simply overlook the procedure. It might want to avoid incurring further expense negotiating over, and potentially litigating, the issue.
- Always ensure that the application is made within the six-month time limit.
- A landlord can use an interim rent application to put more pressure on a tenant who is reluctant to move out.

CHAPTER TWENTY-ONE
DECIDING THE TERMS OF THE NEW TENANCY

Sections 32 to 35 of the LTA 1954 contain provisions dealing with (a) the property to be comprised in the new tenancy; (b) the duration of the term; (c) the rent payable under the new tenancy and (d) all other terms of the new tenancy. The general scheme is that the parties may agree these points, in default of which the court will determine the matter in line with the provisions of sections 32-35 LTA 1954. Any agreement is required by section 69(2) LTA 1954 to be in writing.

New Lease by agreement

Before turning to look at the approach the court takes it is worth bearing in mind that many business tenancies are renewed by agreement; indeed, a great many are renewed without matters becoming contentious or proceedings being commenced at all.

Section 28 LTA 1954 provides that where '*....the landlord and tenant agree to the grant of a future tenancy of the holding, or the holding together with other land, on terms and from a date specified in the agreement, the current tenancy shall continue until that date but no longer and shall not be a tenancy to which Part II applies.*'

'Landlord' in section 28 means 'competent landlord' (see *Bowes-Lyon v Green* [1963] AC 420). There appears to be some doubt as to whether such an agreement needs to be compliant with section 2(1) of the Law of Property (Miscellaneous Provisions Act) 1989 (for reference, see the discussion in Reynolds & Clarke Renewal of Business Tenancies 5th Edition at 15-19 of Laws J's obiter dicta in *Lambert v Keymood* [1997] EGLR 70). A tenant would certainly be unwise to the run the risk of not obtaining a section 2(1) compliant agreement, however, which ought also to be protected by appropriate registration at the Land Registry so as to bind any purchasers of the reversion.

For a discussion of particular issues which may arise in relation to compromising LTA 1954 renewal proceedings, see the treatment of this topic in Foskett on Compromise 9th Edition at 29-12 onwards.

The property to be comprised in the tenancy

Subject to two caveats, and in the absence of agreement, the property to be comprised in the new tenancy is to be the property comprised in the holding, see section 32(1) LTA 1954. The holding, as we have seen, is defined by section 23(3) of the Act to be the property comprised in the current tenancy but less any part which is occupied neither by the tenant nor by a person employed by the tenancy for the purposes of a business by which the tenancy attracts the protection of Part II.

The holding is a somewhat elastic concept temporally for these purposes: the court is required to take the holding *as at the date of its order for a new tenancy*. It is possible, therefore, for the holding to change between service of a Section 25 Notice (or the making of a Section 26 Request) and the order for a new tenancy.

The two caveats to the general rule that the property to be comprised in the new tenancy is the holding are:

1) the landlord has the absolute right by section 32(2) LTA 1954 to insist that the whole of the property comprised in the current tenancy should be included in the grant of the new tenancy; and

2) where the tenant responds to a Ground F case by establishing that there is a smaller, economically severable, part of the holding of which it should be granted a tenancy (*i.e.* without affecting the landlord's development plans) the property to be comprised in the new tenancy will be that severable part.

Section 32(2) LTA 1954 provides that any rights enjoyed under the current tenancy in connection with the holding shall be included within the grant of the new tenancy; these will be real property rights such as easements.

Length of term

The parties are free to agree whatever length of term they wish. Absent such agreement, the court will determine the matter subject to a maximum duration, in the case of a fixed term, of 15 years, see section 33 LTA 1954.

In theory, a periodic tenancy can be ordered although this is rare.

The Act does not itself set down a menu of factors for consideration; rather, it provides that the tenancy to be granted shall be such tenancy as the court considers "reasonable in all the circumstances". This will necessarily be a fact sensitive but some guidance can be suggested as to the type of approach the court is likely to take.

1. First, the length of the current term is likely to be relevant, if only as a starting point.

2. Secondly, the landlord's intentions as regards re-development are likely to be given significant weight. There are a series of decisions in which the courts have made clear that the Act should not operate as an impediment on development. For example, in *Adams v Green and another* [1978] 2 EGLR 46, Stamp LJ held "*that it was no part of the policy--and I underline the word "policy"--of the 1954 Act to give security of tenure to a business tenant at the expense of preventing redevelopment*". In *Reohorn and Another v Barry Corporation* [1956] 1 WLR 845, where the landlord was unable to demonstrate it had the immediate intention to redevelop but desired to do so in due course, the Court of Appeal considered an 8 month fixed term thereafter determinable on six months notice appropriate. (It is worth noting, however, that in *Reohorn* the tenant appears to have accepted that he would not stand in the way if and when the landlord was able to develop).

3. Thirdly, the tenant's business needs and desire for stability are plainly relevant. When redevelopment is a possibility, there can clearly be some conflict between the interests of the tenant (for security) and the landlord (for flexibility to obtain possession). The approach of the court is well illustrated by the decision of the Court of Appeal in *J.H. Edwards & Son Limited v Central London*

Commercial Estates Limited 1984 WL 282810, where the court was concerned not to impede a superior landlord's prospects of developing in due course. Fox LJ described the court's task as follows:

> *In considering what would be proper leases in the circumstances of this case I think that the predominant considerations are two. First, that so far as reasonable the lease should not prevent the superior landlord from using the premises for the purposes of development. Secondly, that a reasonable degree of security of tenure should be provided for the tenants. Those considerations are to some degree in conflict. The function of the court is to strike a reasonable balance between them in all the circumstances of the case.*

In that case, the balance was struck by the Court of Appeal reducing the length of the term to be granted to 7 years and introducing a redevelopment break operative after 5 years: this way the tenant obtained a degree of security of tenure but development possibilities were kept alive.

It does not appear that the landlord needs to prove development is probable; a possibility is sufficient. However, from a practical standpoint, the more the landlord can amass by way of evidence as to the development potential of the property the better placed it will be to resist a lengthy term (or support the inclusion of a favourable break clause).

4. Fourthly, the landlord's intentions as regards its own wishes to use the property (say for its own business occupation) are also relevant. Where the landlord has narrowly missed out on being able to deploy Ground G because of the '5-year rule' (as to which, see Chapter 18), this can be relevant in fixing a relatively short term, see *Wig Creations Ltd v Colour Film Services Ltd* (1969) 20 P & CR 870. In that case, the landlord had purchased its interest 3 years previously but wished to occupy the premises for its own purposes; the five-year rule precluded the landlord from relying on Ground G on the renewal which was before the Court, but the landlord contended that the term to be granted should be no longer than 2 years, by which point it would have clocked up the 5 year period

of ownership necessary to rely on Ground G on any further renewal. The tenant, by contrast, wanted a 12-year term. The Judge considered the five-year period was a relevant factor and decided a 3-year term was appropriate. In dismissing the appeal Lord Denning MR considered the issue on the following basis:

> "*Suppose a landlord bought five years ago, plus one day. He could resist a new tenancy altogether on the ground that he wanted the place for his own business. Suppose he buys it five years ago less one day. Should he be kept out of the place for several years simply by the two-day difference? I think not. The policy of the Act is to give a landlord (who has purchased more than five years ago) an absolute right to get possession for his own business: leaving it to the court to do what is reasonable if he has purchased less than five years. In doing what is reasonable, the five-year period is a factor which it is permissible for the judge to take into account. The weight of it is for him.*" It seems clear, however, that this factor cannot properly operate as an automatic ceiling on the length of the new term; rather it is one (albeit, most likely, powerful) powerful consideration for the judge to consider: see the judgment, in particular, of Edmund Davies LJ in *Wig*.

Commencement date

In the absence of agreement, the new tenancy is to commence following the termination of the continuation tenancy. In the case of an application to court it is likely that the outcome will only be known sometime after the date for termination specified in Section 25 Notice or Section 26 Request, in which case section 64(1) LTA 1954 provides for continuation of the tenancy for a period of 3 months running to the final disposal of the application. 'Final disposal' occurs when the proceedings are determined (including, if there is one, on appeal) and any time for appealing has expired, see section 64(2) LTA 1954. Because of uncertainties as to whether there will be an appeal, it will be apparent that when the court makes its order it will not know precisely when the continuation tenancy will terminate and, therefore, when any new tenancy order ought to commence: the solution to this is to provide in the order for there to be the grant of a new tenancy to commence from the final disposal of the proceedings, and to provide a specified date for the end date of the new tenancy.

Section 36 LTA 1954 contains mechanics for the grant of the new tenancy. The tenant is also afforded an opportunity to change its mind: by section 36(2) LTA 1954 the tenant can, within 14 days from the date the court makes its order for the grant of a new tenancy, apply to the court for the order to be revoked. If such an application is made, the court has no discretion it must order revocation; any orders for costs stand in the absence of any order to the contrary but the court is specifically empowered to revisit costs in the event of revocation. In the event of revocation the continuation tenancy ceases to be a tenancy to which Part II applies; absent agreement between the parties, the court fixes a date for termination allowing the landlord a reasonable time to re-let or otherwise dispose of the premises which would have been comprised in the new tenancy (section 36(2) LTA 1954).

Length of term: chains of tenancies

As we have seen, it maybe that the competent landlord is not the tenant's immediate landlord and there is an intermediate tenant (or tenants) – referred to in the Act as a "mesne landlord" – between the competent landlord on the one hand and the tenant seeking renewal on the other. Schedule 6 LTA 1954 deals with the position regarding agreements for future tenancies and empowers the competent landlord to reach an agreement which will bind the interest of any mesne landlord (see paragraph 3, 6th schedule); however, unless the mesne landlord has consented to the agreement, he is entitled to compensation for any loss suffered (see paragraph 4, 6th Schedule, which also contains provision requiring the mesne landlord to act reasonably in deciding whether to consent).

Where the competent landlord is itself a tenant it maybe that the term the court decides to grant exceeds the remainder of the competent landlord's term. In this case, the court has power to order the grant of such reversionary tenancies as may be necessary, see Schedule 6 to the LTA 1954 which contain the provisions dealing with the grant of new tenancies. (These provisions are of some complexity and repay reading in full. Paragraph 5 of Schedule 6 precludes the competent landlord reaching any agreement which would operate after the expiration of its own interest – *i.e.* so such a landlord cannot bind a superior landlord without its agreement).

Rent

If the parties cannot agree the rent then the court determines the matter. The court has 'regard to the terms of the tenancy (other than those relating to rent)' in deciding the appropriate rent. The task is to ascertain the rent at which the holding might reasonably be expected to be let on the open market by a willing lessor with certain statutory disregard being applied in the valuation exercise, see section 34(1) LTA 1954.

Because the valuation can be affected by the terms of the new tenancy, and indeed the court is specifically required to have "regard to" the terms of the tenancy, the valuation should only be arrived at once the terms are known. This may have an effect on the proper case management of the claim with the valuation exercise coming at a later hearing once the terms are ascertained (unless any disputed terms are unlikely to have an impact on rental value). Alternatively, the surveyor(s) will need to factor in adjustments to their valuations based on different permutations as to the likely terms of the new tenancy.

Expert evidence is usually required; it is important to instruct a valuer with good knowledge of the locality in which the premises are located.

The statutory disregards are set out in section 34 LTA 1954:

a) Any effect on rent of the fact that the tenant has or his predecessors in title have been in occupation of the holding.

b) Any goodwill attached to the holding by reason of the carrying on thereat of the business of the tenant (whether by him or a predecessor of his in that business).

c) Any effect on rent of an improvement to which this paragraph applies.

d) In the case of a holding comprising licensed premises, any addition to its value attributable to the licence, if it appears to the court that having regard to the terms of the current tenancy and any other relevant circumstances the benefit of the licence belongs to the tenant.

Other terms

The parties can agree whatever other terms they wish. In default of agreement the court will determine the terms and in so doing the court '*shall have regard to the terms of the current tenancy and to all the relevant circumstances*', see section 35(1) LTA 1954.

By section 35(2) LTA 1954, '*all the relevant circumstances*' specifically includes the operation of the Landlord and Tenant (Covenants) Act 1995. The 1995 Act represented a '*sea change*' in the law regarding original tenant liability on assignment by providing for the release of the assignor (and its guarantor). Any LTA 1954 renewal tenancy granted after the coming into force of the 1995 Act will be a "new tenancy" for the purposes of the 1995 Act. Neuberger J (as he then was) provided a detailed consideration of section 35(2) LTA 1954 in *Wallis Fashion Group Ltd v CGU Life Assurance Ltd* [2000] 2 EGLR 49. The contest in that case concerned the alienation provisions to be included on renewal, and whether the landlord could insist on a term which would have automatically required the provision of an authorised guarantee agreement ('AGA') on assignment; given the terms of the 1995 Act, Neuberger J considered that a term entitling the landlord to such a guarantee automatically ought not be introduced but, rather, the appropriate term to be included was a term allowing the landlord to require an AGA if it was reasonable to do so.

The leading case on deciding the '*other terms*' of the lease remains the decision of the House of Lords in *O'May v City of London Real Property Co Ltd* [1983] 2 AC 726, in which the landlord sought to modernise the terms of the lease on renewal. The old lease had a rent which was on an "all-inclusive" basis whereas the landlord wanted to move to a more modern, institutional lease, arrangement which provided for a lower rent but with the tenant paying, in addition, a variable service charge (referred to in the decision as a 'clear lease'). The evidence suggested this would have made the landlord's reversion considerably more valuable, as having a known and predictable rental stream, which would not be affected by having to defray the variable costs of repair and service provision, was more attractive to investors. The effect would also, however, to have been to shift the risk of fluctuations in the costs of repair/service provision to the tenants.

The House of Lords decided in favour of the tenants that the landlord had not made out the case for changing the terms from those of the existing lease. The reasoning was as follows:

a) the starting point is the terms of the existing lease;

b) the burden for showing there should be a departure from those terms lies on the party contending for the alteration; in *Gold v Brighton Corporation* [1956] 3 All ER 442 (cited by Lord Wilberforce in *O'May*). Denning LJ considered '*strong and cogent evidence*' would be required to justify the new term sought in that case which would have curtailed one of the tenant's lines of business;

c) the change proposed "*....must in the circumstances of the case, be fair and reasonable, and should take into account, amongst other things, the comparatively weak negotiating position of a sitting tenant requiring renewal, particularly in conditions of scarcity, and the general purpose of the Act which is to protect the business interests of the tenant so far as they are affected by the approaching termination of the current lease, in particular as regards his security of tenure*" (per Lord Hailsham in *O'May*).

A good indication that the exercise is fact sensitive is demonstrated by the case *Edwards & Walkden (Norfolk) Ltd and others v Mayor and others* [2012] EWHC 2527 (Ch) where the court needed to consider the same issue as in *O'May* (*i.e.* whether there should be a shift to a "clear lease" from an all-inclusive rent) but came to the opposite conclusion. Sales J applied the ratio from *O'May* but held that the landlord had, on the particular facts, justified the proposed change. (The tenants in *Edwards* were long-term occupants who had previously occupied under clear leases; there had been a change to an all-inclusive rent during a period when the landlord was carrying out redevelopment works at the market site where the tenants held stalls but it appeared the long-term intention was for there to be a return to a clear lease arrangement. Additionally, the tenants, as users of the particular services in question in that case, were reasonably placed to control fluctuations in the cost of service provision).

As to the approach the court takes to the introduction of a break clause to allow for development, see the discussion above under '*duration of term*'.

CHAPTER TWENTY-TWO

COMPENSATION FOR IMPROVEMENTS UNDER THE LANDLORD AND TENANT ACT 1927 AND DILAPIDATIONS

In the midst of the renewal process these two (distinct) topics can often be overlooked, or only considered late on in the process as somewhat of an afterthought. Each of these matters, however, can be of significant financial importance and they should be borne in mind when advising parties approaching the end of a business tenancy.

Compensation for improvements under the Landlord and Tenant Act 1927

In certain circumstances, and subject to compliance with a series of strict procedural hurdles, business tenants can obtain compensation for improvements they, or their predecessors in title, carried out to their holding. The provisions are contained in Part I of the Landlord and Tenant Act 1927 ('the LTA 1927').

The provisions apply to 'holdings' where the premises comprised in the holding are held under a lease and used '*wholly or partly for the carrying on thereat any trade or business*', see section 17 LTA 1927. Certain tenancies are excluded: mining leases; agricultural holdings; farm-business tenancies and tenancies held by the tenant as a result of any office, appointment or employment with the landlord, see section 17 LTA 1927 generally.

'Lease' is defined in section 25(1) LTA 1927 to include an underlease, or an assignment operating as a lease or underlease; it also extends to an agreement for a lease, underlease or assignment operating as a lease/underlease.

Whilst there are some similarities between the tenancies to which Part I of LTA 1927 on the one hand and Part II of LTA 1954 on the other apply (*i.e.* both, very broadly speaking, apply to 'business' tenants) there are important differences. For example:

a) Part I of LTA 1927 applies where the premises are used wholly or in part for '*carrying on thereat any trade or business*'. However, there are no provisions requiring this to be the tenant's business; compare this with the need for the tenant to be in occupation for the purposes of a business carried on by the tenant under section 23 of LTA 1954.

b) Section 17 LTA 1927 makes explicit that '*any trade or business*' is deemed to include the regular carrying on of a 'profession'. However, the types of activity which can qualify as a 'trade or business' for the LTA 1927 would appear to be somewhat narrower than under Part II of the LTA 1954.

c) Whilst both regimes require a tenancy, there is no minimum length in respect of fixed terms for the 1927 Act: there is no equivalent in the LTA 1927 of the LTA 1954 requirement that a fixed term need be at least 6 months in duration. As with Part II of LTA 1954, however, periodic tenancies *are* included.

d) There is no concept of 'competent landlord' under the LTA 1927.

Since changes to the LTA 1927 in 1953 it has not been possible for the parties to contract out of its operation.

<u>The scheme</u>

There are 3 stages at which Part I of the LTA 1927 needs to be considered:

a) prior the tenant carrying out the works ("Stage 1");

b) prior to and around the time of termination of the tenancy ("Stage 2"); and

c) following the tenant quitting the holding ("Stage 3").

A tenant who follows the correct procedures, and time limits, at each stage may obtain compensation in certain circumstances.

Stage 1: Prior to works being carried out

Section 2(1) of the LTA 1927 creates a number of exclusions to the right to compensation in certain cases, but these need to be read alongside section 48 LTA 1954. Section 2(1)(b) specifically excludes building leases (along with other improvement which the tenant or his predecessors in title were under an obligation to make in pursuance of a contract entered into for valuable consideration): this exclusion remains in force. The exception in respect of any improvement made in pursuance of a statutory obligation (section 2(1)(b)) was disapplied in respect of improvements begun after the LTA 1954 came into force on 1 October 1954 (section 48(1) LTA 1954). The exclusions that improvements made less than three years before the termination of the tenancy are also excluded (section 2(1)(c)) and that the landlord can offer a renewal tenancy instead (section 2(1)(d)) were also disapplied by section 48(2) and (3) respectively after the LTA 1954 came into force.

By section 3 of LTA 1927, a tenant to whom that part applies can set in train a procedure potentially entitling him to carry out works of improvement irrespective of any covenants in the lease embargoing such works.

The procedure requires the tenant to serve on the immediate landlord a notice setting out the proposed works, together with a plan and specification: section 3 (1) LTA 1927. There is no prescribed form and a letter will suffice providing it is sufficiently clear the Acts provisions are being invoked, including putting the landlord on notice that there will be a liability for compensation at the end of the tenancy (see *Deerfield Travel Services Ltd v Wardens and Society of the Mistery or Art of the Leathersellers of the City of London* (1983) 46 P & CR 132 generally); a document as opposed to oral notification, however, is required, section 23 LTA 1927.

Once the landlord is in receipt of the tenant's request he has 3 months within which to object by written notice; again, there is no prescribed form. The landlord also has the right, within the 3-month period, to notify the tenant that he will carry out the works in return for an increase in rent. If the landlord does not respond within the 3-month period, the tenant becomes entitled to carry out the works in accordance with his plan and specification.

If the immediate landlord is himself a tenant it is important that he passes on all documents relating to the improvements to his own landlord: the LTA 1927 contains provisions for mesne landlords to seek reimbursement at the end of his term of any compensation he has to pay his own tenant but this is subject to having kept his own landlord properly informed in the manner required by section 8 of the LTA 1927, and a claim for reimbursement being made in accordance with that section (essentially, within 2 months before the expiration of his term).

If there is a dispute between the tenant and landlord as to the entitlement to carry out the works, then an application to the 'tribunal' can be made by the tenant. The 'tribunal' is the High Court or County Court; it is suggested, however, that it would be extremely rare for such proceedings to be appropriate for the High Court and the County Court is most likely to be the most appropriate forum. Procedurally, CPR 56 and the Practice Direction to that part set out how the claim should proceed.

If the court is satisfied the works are proper works within the LTA 1927, it will certify that fact by order. If the court is not so satisfied, then a certificate will not be granted. The court can also certify varied works as being proper improvements. Finally, the court can decline a certificate on the basis the landlord has offered to carry out the works for an increase in rent.

There is no definition of 'improvement' within the LTA 1927 but section 3(1) provides that for a certificate to be given by the court that the improvement is a proper improvement it must:

a) be of such a nature as to be calculated to add to the letting value of the holding at the termination of the tenancy; and

b) be reasonable and suitable to the character of the holding; and

c) not be such as to diminish the value of any other property belonging to the same landlord or to any superior landlord from whom the immediate landlord of the tenant directly or indirectly holds.

The question of what is an 'improvement' was considered by the Court of Appeal in *Lambert v F W Woolworth & Co Ltd (No 2)* [1938] Ch 883. It should be considered from the point of view of the tenant. It must be limited to an improvement of the demised property. The question is: how can the tenant get the most beneficial use of the premises; or will the alterations render the tenant's occupation of the premises more convenient and comfortable to the tenant. It is immaterial that the alteration may not improve, or even damage, the demised premises from the point of view of the landlord.

To gain the right to compensation in due course, the tenant must complete the works in line with the plan/specification approved (or as amended by agreement or on subsequent application for amendment) and within the timescales proposed. Once the works are complete, the tenant can request the landlord to certify the works have been properly completed; if the landlord fails to give such a certificate within 1 month the tenant can make an application to court for the court to certify the works have been properly complete, see section 1 of the LTA 1927.

The landlord (or court) certificate that the works have been completed properly is not a pre-requisite to a claim for compensation in due course. The tenant would be well advised, however, to obtain such a certificate to prevent arguments further down the line. As a tenant can rely on works carried out by a predecessor in title it would be worthwhile if taking an assignment of the residue of a term to check whether any LTA 1927 Act works have been carried out by the assignor (or his predecessors in title) and to obtain any certificates the assignor may have in his possession.

Stage 2: At/around the time of termination

The actual entitlement to compensation arises on the tenant quitting the premises. However, prior to that, a written claim is required to have been made by the tenant (save as regards forfeiture/re-entry in which case the claim is made within a certain period post termination). Failure to make such a claim in time and in the correct form will preclude the tenant's entitlement in due course to compensation. Note, this written claim is *not* the making of a *court* claim at this stage; that comes later.

Section 1 LTA 1927 refers the reader to section 47 LTA 1954 for the time-limits for submitting a written claim at this stage. The claim needs to be in writing and, crucially, needs (amongst other requirements) to state the amount of compensation claimed.

By section 1 LTA 1927 the amount of compensation shall not exceed:

a) the net addition to the value of the holding as a whole which may be determined to be the direct result of the improvement; or

b) the reasonable cost of carrying out the improvement at the termination of the tenancy, subject to a deduction of an amount equal to the cost (if any) of putting the works constituting the improvement into a reasonable state of repair, except so far as such cost is covered by liability of the tenant under any covenant or agreement as to the repair of the premises.

Regard is had to the intended use for the premises following the termination of the tenancy, and to any plans to alter or demolish the premises: so, if (say) the landlord intends to demolish the building and will gain no benefit from the improvement, no compensation will be payable.

There are a variety of ways the tenancy might come to an end and section 47 LTA 1954 deals with these as follows. It is very important to note the statutory time limits, as many of them run from the date that a notice is given: it is easy to overlook them.

a) If the tenancy is terminated by notice to quit, or notice under Part 1 or Part II of the 1927 Act or Part II of the LTA 1954 then the claim needs to be made within 3 months <u>from the date such notice is given</u> (save that as regards the service of a Section 26 Request by the tenant the 3 month period runs from the giving of the landlord's counter-notice or, if the landlord fails to serve a counter-notice the latest date on which he could have given such notice).

b) If the tenancy determines by effluxion of time, then the claim must be made not earlier than 6 nor later than 3 months before the coming to the end of the tenancy.

c) If the tenancy is terminated for forfeiture / re-entry, then the claim must be made within 3 months from the effective date of the order or (in the case of peaceable re-entry without court order, the date of re-entry). The 'effective date of the order' means the later of the date specified for possession or the time for appealing.

The written claim must be made in the prescribed manner which is currently as set out in the Civil Procedure Rules 1998 ("CPR") PD 56 at paragraph 5.8. It must be in writing, signed by the claimant, his solicitor or agent and include details of:

1. the name and address of the claimant and of the landlord against whom the claim is made;

2. the property to which the claim relates;

3. the nature of the business carried on at the property;

4. a concise statement of the nature of the claim;

5. particulars of the improvement, including the date it was completed and the costs; and

6. the amount claimed.

A mesne landlord must immediately serve a copy of the claim on his immediate superior landlord and so on up the chain (if there is a chain) to the freeholder: this is important to ensure compliance with section 8 to enable the mesne landlord to make an onward claim up the chain for compensation payable at the end of his term.

<u>Stage 3: the actual court claim</u>

The cause of action is only complete after the tenant has quit.

Thereafter, the tenant who has managed to jump through the hoops above has a claim to compensation in accordance with section 1 LTA 1927. If the amount cannot be agreed it is determined by the court.

Again, CPR Part 56 and PD 56 apply procedurally as regards such a claim.

Tips

- Make your clients aware of Part 1 LTA 1927 in good time.
- Remember the LTA 1927 can be used to outflank even an outright prohibition on carrying out works.
- Obtain an appropriate certificate to show the works have been carried out properly so as to prevent argument later on.
- If taking an assignment of a term, ascertain if the assignor has carried out works to which the LTA 1927 applies and if so obtain documentary evidence the procedures to that date have been followed.
- Be alive to the time limits at each of the three stages. Be aware of the period for making a claim once a notice is given under the LTA 1954. Plan early.

Dilapidations

A full discussion of the law on dilapidations is outside the scope of this text. The law is complex and nuanced and the reader is referred to specialist practitioner works in the area, such as *Dowding & Reynolds: Dilapidations, The Modern Law and Practice (6th Edition, Sweet & Maxwell)*. The following general points, however, are worth flagging in the context of LTA 1954 Act claims:

- Dilapidations claims can be extremely costly and time consuming. Tenants should plan early to minimise exposure. A decent building surveyor will most often be needed. It is often cheaper for the tenant to arrange for any necessary works to be carried out prior to the end of the tenancy, rather than facing a large claim in relation to dilapidations (including a claim for any loss of rent as a result of the landlord being unable to re-let the property whilst it carries out any necessary works). If possible an agreed schedule of works should be negotiated and carried out in good time.

- The strategy for landlord and tenant will, no doubt, be affected by whether the tenant wants, and the landlord is prepared to grant, a new tenancy. If there is agreement, then consideration may be given to a schedule of works being annexed to the new lease.

- If the tenant is seeking to renew and there is any risk that the landlord might seek to rely on Ground A (want of repair) the need to put the property into good repair in good time (and by the time of the hearing) will obviously be of importance.

- If the landlord is seeking to oppose a new tenancy (or seek termination) on Ground F attention should be focused on the extent to which the development plans cut down any exposure for the tenant to a dilapidations claim. In particular, attention should be paid to section 18(1) of the LTA 1927, which places a cap (by reference to the diminution in value of the reversion) on the damages a landlord can seek in respect of want of repair. So if, say, the landlord intends to demolish the whole of the building containing the demised premises the diminution in value of its reversion as a result of any want of repair will be zero.

- If the landlord is seeking to oppose a new tenancy on Grounds F (redevelopment) *and* A (want of repair), the tenant can find itself in a serious tactical dilemma: on the one hand, the desire to defeat the Ground A ground of opposition suggests the tenant should carry out repairs prior to the hearing; on the other hand, if the landlord makes out Ground F on the basis its plans would mean the demolition or re-construction of the premises.

- Potential liability to a dilapidations claim should be factored into strategic thinking, planning and any settlement. Dependent on the landlord's plans and attitude, a tenant facing a potentially large dilapidations claim may find itself in a position where a settlement involving its surrender of the premises needs to be considered. (In which case regard should be had to provisions in the LTA 1954 on

(a) agreements for surrender (b) agreements as to the amount for compensation – as to which see chapters 3 and 19 respectively).

- Attention should be paid to the Pre-Action Protocol for Claims for Damages in Relation to the Physical State of Commercial Property at Termination of a Tenancy ("the Dilapidations Protocol").

CHAPTER TWENTY-THREE
COURT PROCEDURE

Introduction

There are a number of different scenarios in which proceedings under LTA 1954 may arise. First, the tenant may apply for a new lease pursuant to section 24 (1) following service of a Section 25 Notice by the landlord or the making of a section 26 Request by the tenant. Secondly, following the changes introduced by the 2003 Order, *the landlord* may now make an application for there to be a new tenancy following the tenant making a Section 26 Request (or the landlord serving a Section 25 Notice). Thirdly, the landlord may apply pursuant to section 29(2) for the continuation tenancy to be terminated without the grant of a new tenancy. Additionally, whichever way matters proceed, the landlord (or tenant) may wish to bring a claim for there to be an interim rent.

Procedure rules

The procedural rules are contained in Civil Procedure Rules ('CPR') Part 56 and its Practice Direction, PD 56. References below are to the current version of the rules and, in particular, to the regime which has applied from 1st June 2004 when the 2003 Order came into effect.

Pilot Scheme

At the time of writing, the County Court at Central London is still operating a pilot scheme under which unopposed business lease renewal claims are allocated to the Property Chamber of the First-tier Tribunal ('FTT').

The County Court at Central London has also promulgated draft directions for unopposed lease renewals (on Form BLR1) and opposed lease renewals (on Form BLR3), while the FTT has also issued standard directions for unopposed lease renewals (Form DR1) which should be consulted, although like all template directions, these should be adapted to the needs of the individual case.

The PACT scheme

The Royal Institution of Chartered Surveyors ('RICS') and the Law Society have established an out of court process for the determination of all or some of the terms of a renewal lease through arbitration or expert determination, called Professional Arbitration on Court Terms ('PACT'). The PACT scheme can be used pre-issue or post-issue, although parties engaging the scheme pre-issue should still be alert to the statutory time limits for court applications which are not disapplied. The Law Society and RICS have issued a useful joint guidance note on tenancy renewals under PACT. The operation of PACT falls outside the scope of this book, but parties and practitioners are alerted to the possibility of using this scheme or other forms of Alternative Dispute Resolution ('ADR').

Opposed versus unopposed claims

The CPR draw a fundamental distinction between 'an unopposed claim' for a new tenancy on the one hand and an 'opposed claim' on the other. The two different categories of claim have different procedural needs and attract different treatment in the rules.

An '*unopposed claim'* means:

> "*..a claim for a new tenancy under section 24 of the 1954 Act in circumstances where the grant of a new tenancy is not opposed*", see CPR 56.3 (2) (b) and PD 56 para 3.1 (1).

An '*opposed claim*' means:

> '*...a claim for –*
>
> *(a) a new tenancy under section 24 of the 1954 Act in circumstances where the grant of a new tenancy is opposed; or*
>
> *(b) the termination of a tenancy under section 29 (2) of the 1954 Act*', see CPR 56.3 (2) (c) and PD 56 para 3.1 (2).

As regards opposed claims, PD 56 para 3.1(3) defines 'grounds of opposition' to encompass not only the grounds on which the landlord may oppose under section 30(1) of LTA 1954 (*i.e.* the 7 grounds dealt with in Chapters 11-18) but also '*any other basis on which the landlord asserts that a new tenancy ought not to be granted*'. It seems likely the latter encompasses the scenario where it is said that the tenant is not entitled in principle to a new tenancy, *i.e.* where the tenant is alleged not to be in occupation for the purpose of a business.

Starting the claim: High Court or County Court (and which Hearing Centre)?

Both the High Court and the County Court have concurrent jurisdiction under the LTA 1954 in relation to claims for a new tenancy (or termination): section 63 of the Act. High Court claims are rare.

CPR 56.2(2) provides that the claim may be commenced in the High Court if the claimant files a certificate stating the reasons for so doing, verified by statement of truth. 56.2 PD paras 2.3 to 2.6 deal with issuing in the High Court and provide that only '*exceptional circumstances*' justify such a course.

Circumstances which '*may, in an appropriate case*' justify commencing proceedings in the High Court are complicated disputes of fact, or points of general importance being involved, see 56.2 PD para 2.4. The value of the property and any financial claim '*may*' be relevant circumstances but will not normally be sufficient of themselves to justify commencing in the High Court, see para 2.5 of the Practice Direction. If the claim is brought in the High Court it must be brought in the Chancery division: PD 56 para 2.6.

Paragraph 2.3 of the Practice Direction provides that if the claim is wrongly commenced in the High Court the court will normally either strike out the claim or transfer the proceedings to the County Court. The Practice Direction makes the point that this is likely to result in delay and that the court would normally disallow the costs of commencing in the High Court and transfer in these circumstances.

Where the claim is made in the County Court, the practical effect of CPR 56.2(1) and PD 56.2 is that the claim may be made in any County Court Hearing Centre. If that Centre is not the Centre which serves the address where the property is situated, however, the claim will be transferred following issue to the Centre which does serve that address. PD 56.2 para

2.2 (2) makes clear that the claimant should therefore '*...consider the potential delay which may result if a claim is not sent to the appropriate County Court Centre in the first place*'. Unless there is a tactical reason to actively court delay, it is therefore suggested that the Claimant should make the claim in the appropriate hearing Centre in the first place.

Issuing the claim: Part 8 or Part 7?

Where the claim is an unopposed claim, and there is accordingly no dispute that there should be a new tenancy, the claim must be commenced by using the Part 8 procedure using the Part 8 Claim Form (i.e. Form 208), see CPR r 5.3(3).

Rules 8.5 and 8.5 of the Part 8 procedure, dealing with service of evidence, are specifically dis-applied: the Claimant and Defendant do not, therefore, serve their evidence with the Claim Form and Acknowledgement of Service respectively; rather, they await directions from the court which are given following the service of the Defendant's acknowledgement of service, see CPR r 56.3(3)(c).

Where the claim is an opposed claim, the Part 7 procedure must be adopted using the Part 7 claim form, N1.

Time limit for applying to court

The claim for a new tenancy under section 24 (1) (or termination under section 29 (2)) must be brought within the 'statutory period' provided for by section 29 A of LTA 1954, otherwise the court 'shall not entertain' the claim.

Where the landlord gives a notice under Section 25, the statutory period ends on the date specified in that notice, see section 29A (2) (a) LTA 1954. Where the tenant makes a request under Section 26 for a new tenancy the period ends immediately before the date specified in the Section 26 notice, see section 29 A (2) (b); it appears, therefore, that a claim made *on* the day specified in the Section 26 notice would be too late. This inconsistency would appear to present a potential trap. In any event, parties would be well advised not to leave matters until the dying light of the end of the statutory period.

Where the tenant has made a request under Section 26, a claim for a new tenancy cannot be made before the expiry of 2 months beginning with the date the request was made, unless the landlord has served a counter-notice under section 26(6) stating he will oppose the grant of a new tenancy.

The 'statutory period' may be extended by agreement between the landlord and tenant providing the agreement complies with the requirements of the Act. Any such agreement must be made in writing, see section 69(2) LTA 1954. The agreement must be made within the statutory period and specify the new date by which the application must be made, see section 29(B). Successive agreements can be made, providing they are in writing and specify the new period.

It is vital, particularly for the tenant, not to miss the date by which the claim must be brought as the court has no power to extend the statutory period. Tenants should be careful not to be misled into missing the deadline by unconcluded negotiations for a new tenancy: the tenant should always either seek a concrete agreement with the landlord, within the statutory period, for an extension or issue a protective claim in good time.

When must service be effected?

It was previously the case, prior to 1 October 2008, that a claim form in Part II proceedings only had a 'shelf life' of 2 months; service was required within that period as opposed to the ordinary position of 4 months under the CPR. This was also a trap for the unwary.

From the 1 October 2008, however, the 2-month provision has been abolished and the standard provisions in the CPR 7.5 apply: the Claimant therefore has 4 months to effect service.

Pre-action protocol behaviour, negotiations and tactics

There is no bespoke pre-action protocol for Part II claims. Given the absence of a bespoke protocol, reference should also be made to the general Pre-Action Protocol in the CPR (and to guidance published by professional associations such as the Property Litigation Association).

The pre-action behaviour expected will differ between 'opposed' and 'unopposed' claims.

There is, now, no automatic ability to obtain a stay for negotiation built into the rules; however, either party may apply for such a stay.

Precedence of competing claims where the landlord and tenant bring claims under section 24(1)/29 (2)

The rules need to be understood against the backcloth of the following provisions of the LTA 1954 itself:

a) Section 24(2A) LTA 1954 provides that neither the landlord nor tenant may make an application for a new tenancy if the other has made such an application and served the same.

b) Section 24(2B) LTA 1954 provides that neither the tenant (nor landlord) may make an application for there to be a new tenancy if the landlord has applied for termination under section 29 (2) LTA 1954 and served the same;

c) If the landlord has got in first, whether by making a claim that there should be a new tenancy, or bringing a claim for termination, the landlord may not withdraw the same without the consent of the tenant (see sections 29(6) and 29(2C) respectively).

It will be apparent that sections 24 (2A) and (2B) LTA 1954 refer to claims which have been both 'made' and 'served'. There may be situations, however, where there is a delay before service and, during that period, the other party issues (and, perhaps, then serves) a claim. There are a number of permutations. PD 56 para 3.2 seeks to regulate the position. The rules are designed to ensure that the substance of the dispute gets before the court in an orderly fashion without the tenant being prejudiced by a landlord commencing, and then not pursuing, a claim tactically to lure the tenant into not bringing a claim within the strict time limits provided by the Act.

In summary:

a) Once an application under section 24(1) LTA 1954 has been served on the defendant, no further application in respect of the same tenancy, whether for a new tenancy under section 24(1) or for termination under section 29(2), may be made by the Defendant without permission of the court.

b) If more than one application under section 24 (1) is *served* on the same day, any landlord's application shall stand stayed until further order of the court.

c) If applications are *served* on the same day and one is by the tenant under section 24 (1) LTA 1954 for a new tenancy and the other is by the landlord under section 29 (2) LTA 1954 for termination, the landlord's claim takes precedence and the tenant's claim is stayed until further order of the court. The landlord's claim will then proceed: if the landlord succeeds, there will be no new tenancy and the continuation tenancy will terminate in accordance with section 64 of the Act. If, however, the landlord fails on the termination application those proceedings will be the vehicle for the tenant to obtain the grant of a new tenancy. Then landlord cannot withdraw without the tenant's consent: section 29(6) LTA 1954.

d) If the tenant has issued, but not served, a claim under section 24(1) for a new tenancy and the landlord issues and serves a claim under section 29(2) for termination, the landlord's claim is treated as a deemed notice under CPR 7.7 requiring the tenant to either serve or discontinue the tenant's claim within 14 days of service of the landlord's claim.

Contents of the Claim form: all cases

PD para 3.4 provides that in all cases (i.e. whether the claim is under section 24(1) for a new tenancy or under section 29(1) for termination, and whether the claim is 'opposed' or 'unopposed') the claim form must contain details of:

1. the property to which the claim relates;

2. the particulars of the current tenancy (including date, parties and duration), the current rent (if not the original rent) and the date and method of termination;

3. every notice or request given or made under sections 25 or 26 of the LTA 1954; and

4. the expiry date of –

    (a) the statutory period under section 29A(2) LTA 1954; or

    (b) any agreed extended period made under section 29B(1) or 29B(2) of LTA 1954.

The Practice Direction then goes on to set out additional details that are required for the claim form dependent upon the nature of the claim and by whom it is brought.

Requirements for the claim form: tenant making a claim for a new tenancy

This may be an unopposed or opposed claim, dependent on the landlord's attitude. As we have seen above, if the claim is *unopposed* the tenant must use the Part 8 procedure; the effect of CPR 8.2 is that the tenant must state on the claim form (i) that the claim is made under Landlord and Tenant Act 1954 and (ii) state the remedy sought.

Whether opposed or unopposed, in addition to the details required by PD 56 para 3.4, PD 56 para 3.5 provides that the claim for must contain details of:

1. the nature of the business carried out at the property;

2. whether the claimant relies on section 23(1A), 41 or 42 and, if so, the basis on which he does so (these are the controlling interest company provisions, trust provisions and group company provisions respectively);

3. whether the claimant relies on section 31A of the 1954 Act and, if so, the basis on which he does so (the tenant may wish to consider

whether the deploy these provisions in response to a Ground F case – as to which see Chapter 17);

4. whether any, and if so what part, of the property comprised in the tenancy is occupied by neither the claimant nor a person employed by the claimant for the purpose of the claimant's business;

5. the claimant's proposed terms for the new tenancy; and

6. the name and address of anyone known to the claimant who (a) has an interest in the reversion in the property (whether immediate or in not more than 15 years) on the termination of the claimant's current tenancy and who is likely to be affected by the grant of a new tenancy; or (b) if the claimant does not know of anyone specified in (a) then anyone who has a freehold interest in the property. [Additionally, the claim form must be served on these categories of person – see PD 56 para 3.6].

By PD 56 para 3.3, the person who is the landlord as defined in section 44 of the Act (i.e. the 'competent landlord') must be a defendant.

It is clear from this rule that the claim form will be full of details, even where the Part 7 procedure applies.

Requirements for the claim form: landlord making claim for a new tenancy

By definition this will be an unopposed claim and the landlord will, therefore, be using the Part 8 procedure. The claimant will need to specify that the claim is made pursuant to the Landlord and Tenant Act 1954 and the remedy sought.

In addition to the details required by PD 56 para 3.4, where the landlord is making the claim that there be a new tenancy PD 56 para 3.7 requires the claim form to give details of:

1. the claimant's proposed terms for the new tenancy;

2. whether the claimant is aware that the defendant's tenancy is one to which section 32(2) applies (*i.e.* where the tenancy includes property other than the holding) and if so whether the claimant

requires that any new tenancy shall be a tenancy of the whole of the property comprised in the tenancy or just the holding;

3. the name and address of anyone known to the claimant who (a) has an interest in the reversion in the property (whether immediate or in not more than 15 years) on the termination of the claimant's current tenancy and who is likely to be affected by the grant of a new tenancy; or (b) if the claimant does not know of anyone specified in (a) then anyone who has a freehold interest in the property. As with the position if the tenant makes the claim, any person identified by the requirement to state these details must be served with the claim form – see 56 PD 3.8.

If the tenant in fact does not want a new tenancy, section 29(5) of LTA 1954 provides that: '*if the tenant informs the court that he does not want a new tenancy*' the landlord's application shall be dismissed. There is no prescribed form or procedure and it appears a letter from the tenant will suffice.

Claim form: landlord's application for termination under section 29(2)

In addition to the PD 56 para 3.4 details, where the landlord brings the claim for termination PD 56 para 3.9 provides that the claim form must contain:

1. the claimant's grounds of opposition;

2. full details of those grounds of opposition; and

3. the terms of a new tenancy that the claimant proposes in the event his claim fails.

Acknowledgement of service and (if applicable) defence

PD 56 sets out various details which the defendant must provide. If the claim is an unopposed claim and, therefore, the Part 8 procedure is being used these details must be set out the acknowledgment of service as no defence will be served. If the claim is an opposed claim, the Part 7 procedure will be used and the prescribed details will need to be set out in the Defence.

In each permutation of case, the aim is to have all possible issues flushed out on the statements of case.

Acknowledgement of service: unopposed claim where the claimant is the tenant

PD 56 para 3.10 provides that the landlord's acknowledgement of service must be in form N210 and must state with particulars:

1. whether, if a new tenancy is granted, the defendant objects to any of the terms proposed by the claimant and if so the terms to which he objects and the terms he proposes insofar as they differ from those proposed by the claimant;

2. whether the defendant is a tenant under a lease having less than 15 years unexpired at the date of the termination of the claimant's current tenancy and if so the name and address of any person who, to the knowledge of the defendant, has an interest in the property expectant (whether immediate or in not more than 15 years from that date) on the termination of the tenancy;

3. the name and address of any person having an interest in the property who is likely to be affected by the grant of a new tenancy; and

4. if the claimant's current tenancy is one to which section 32(2) applies, whether the defendant requires any new tenancy shall be a tenancy of the whole of the property comprised in the claimant's tenancy.

Acknowledgement of service where the claim is an unopposed claim for a new tenancy and the claimant is the landlord

Again, the acknowledgement must be in Form N210. PD 56 para 3.11 provides that the acknowledgement must state with particulars:

1. the nature of the business carried on at the property;

2. if the defendant relies on section 23(1A), 41 or 42 LTA 1954 the basis upon which he does so;

3. whether any, and if so what part, of the property comprised in the tenancy is occupied neither by the defendant nor by any person employed by the defendant for the purpose of the defendant's business.

4. the name and address of:

   (a) anyone known to the defendant who has an interest in the reversion in the property (whether immediate of in not more than 15 years) on the termination of the defendant's tenancy and who is likely to be affected by the grant of a new tenancy; or

   (b) if the defendant does not know of anyone within (a) anyone who has a freehold interest in the property;

5. whether, if the tenancy is granted, the defendant objects to any of the terms proposed by the claimant and if so the terms to which objection is taken and the terms he proposes insofar as they differ from those proposed by the claimant.

Acknowledgement of service and defence in an opposed claim where the claimant is the tenant

PD 56 para 3.12 provides that where the claimant in an opposed claim is the tenant the acknowledgement is to be in form N9 (which is the standard acknowledgement of service form for Part 7 Claims). The defendant in fact has a choice as to whether to serve an acknowledgement of service in such a case; whether to do so will depend upon whether the defendant is in a position to serve its defence within 14 days or requires the additional time afforded by service of an acknowledgement. The defendant must state in his defence with particulars:

a) his grounds of opposition;

b) full details of those grounds of opposition;

c) whether, if a new tenancy is granted, the defendant objects to any of the terms proposed by the landlord and if so the terms to which objection is made and the terms the defendant proposes insofar as they differ from those proposed by the claimant;

d) whether the defendant is a tenant under a lease having less than 15 years unexpired at the date of the termination of the claimant's current tenancy and, if so, the name and address of any person who, to the knowledge of the defendant has an interest in the reversion in the property expectant (whether immediately or in not more than 15 years from that date) on the termination of the defendant's tenancy;

e) the name and address of any person having an interest in the property who is likely to be affected by the grant of a new tenancy; and

f) if the claimant's current tenancy is one to which section 32 (2) applies whether the defendant requires that any new tenancy shall be a tenancy of the whole of the property comprised in the claimant's current tenancy.

Acknowledgement of service and defence where the claimant is the landlord making an application for termination under section 29(2) LTA 1954

Last, if the claimant is the landlord seeking an order for termination without the grant of a new tenancy pursuant to section 29(2) LTA 1954, PD 56 para 3.13 provides that the defendant's acknowledgment shall be in form N9; as above, the tenant has the choice as to whether to serve an acknowledgement. The tenant must state in his defence with particulars:

a) whether he relies on sections 23(1A), 41 or 42 LTA 1954 and if so on what basis;

b) whether the defendant relies on section 31A LTA 1954 and if so on what basis; and

c) the terms of the new tenancy the defendant would propose in the event the claimant's claim for termination fails.

Amendments

The CPR applies generally in relation to amendments.

Unopposed claims – general case management and progress

No evidence needs to be filed unless and until the court directs it be filed: PD 56 para 3.14.

As these claims use the Part 8 procedure (albeit, as modified) they are treated as allocated to the multi-track, see CPR 8.9(c).

Directions Questionnaires are not used with Part 8 claims. Directions are usually given on paper, or at a telephone C.M.C.

It is likely that the main issue in these cases will be rent although, of course, there may be dispute as to the other terms of the tenancy. Directions will need to be tailored accordingly.

If the case is proceeding under the Pilot Scheme operated by the County Court at Central London, the case is likely to be transferred to the FTT. The FTT is likely to issue standard directions together with a Listing Questionnaire.

CPR Part 35 deals with the rules on expert evidence in general and restricts its use to that which is "reasonably required" to resolve the proceedings. The court seeks to limit expert evidence, restrict the same to written reports and encourages the use of single joint experts where appropriate. However, parties are regularly granted permission to instruct separate experts on valuation in these cases (unless the rental is modest or the difference between the parties is small).

Opposed claims – general case management and progress

Such a claim will have commenced by the Part 7 procedure. Once a defence is filed, Directions Questionnaires will be dispatched for completion and filing by the parties.

The claim will be allocated by reference to the usual test in CPR 26.8; the choice practically speaking lies between the fast track and multi-track (PD 26 para 8.1 accepts that opposed landlord claims under Part 56 are not generally suitable for the small claims track).

If the claim is to be allocated to the multi-track, costs budgeting will apply unless dispensed with: the reader is referred to the general works on Civil Procedure and costs in relation to the niceties of the costs budgeting process but care should be taken to ensure that time limits for filing budgets are kept to because of the sanctions applicable for non-compliance.

Preliminary issues are the norm in opposed claims: PD 56 para 3.16 provides that unless the circumstances make it unreasonable to do so, any grounds of opposition will be tried first. If a party has raised a challenge as to validity of the Section 25 or Section 26 notice, it is likely that this will be dealt with as a preliminary issue as well.

As set out at the start of this chapter, the Central London at County Court has issued useful draft directions for opposed lease renewals which can be adapted to the needs of the individual case.

Evidence (including expert evidence) will be filed in accordance with the directions of the court but PD 56 para 3.15 provides that the landlord 'shall' be required to file his evidence first.

Costs

Costs are in the discretion of the court: *Decca Navigator v Greater London Council* [1974] 1 W.L.R. 748; see also *Demag Industrial Equipment v Canada Dry (U.K.)* [1969] 1 W.L.R. 985. Where there is a clear 'winner' e.g. where a landlord successfully opposes the grant of a new lease, the tenant will usually be ordered to pay the landlord's costs; and vice versa if the tenant succeeds in such a case. Where rent is in issue, and the judge decides on an intermediate rent, no order for costs will often be the order: *Le Witt v Brookes* [1956] 1 W.L.R. 1438. While in one case where the parties had settled the terms of a proposed statutory tenancy out of court and the judge held that he could not decide who should bear the costs of the application, in a later case where the terms were also settled out of court, Fulford J dismissed an appeal against the decision of the first instance judge who been invited by the parties to determine costs, and who had awarded the tenant its costs on the basis that the landlord had only at the last moment conceded on the major issues in dispute so that the tenant had secured success on the major issues: See *Campion & Bower v. Abbot* [1956] J.P.L. 194; 105 L.J. 684 and cf *MBI Incorporated v Riminex Investments* [2002] EWHC 2856 (QB).

Interim rent

The reader is referred to Chapter 20 dealing with the substance of such applications.

Either the landlord or tenant may make such a claim once the landlord has served a Section 25 Notice or the tenant made a Section 26 request. Neither may make an application for interim rent if the other has made such an application and not withdrawn it. No application may be entertained if made more than 6 months after the termination of the relevant tenancy.

PD 56 paragraphs 3.17 to 3.19 regulate how claims for an interim rent shall be made. Where proceedings have already commenced for the grant of a new tenancy, or termination, then any claim for interim rent under section 24 A LTA 1954 shall be made by (1) the claim form; (2) the acknowledgement of service or defence; or (3) a Part 23 application notice.

Where no proceedings have yet to be commenced, the claim for interim rent is made by way of a Part 8 claim form which shall include details of:

1. the property to which the property relates;

2. the particulars of the relevant tenancy (including date, parties and duration) and the current rent (if not the original rent);

3. every notice or request given or made under sections 25 or 26 LTA 1954;

4. if the relevant tenancy has terminated, the date and mode of terminations;

5. if the relevant tenancy has terminated and the landlord has granted a new tenancy of the property to the tenant – (a) the particulars of the new tenancy (including date, parties and duration) and rent and (b) in a case to which section 24C(2) applies but the claimant

seeks a different rent under section 24C (3), particulars and matters on which the claimant relies as satisfying section 24C(3).

Any application under section 24D(3) LTA 1954 shall be made by Part 23 application: see PD 56 para 3.18.

Procedural Tips Generally

- Diarise dates carefully so as not to miss the deadline for making an application (whether for a new tenancy or for interim rent).

- Make sure any agreement to extend the statutory period is reached in good time formally compliant.

- Ensure you follow reasonable pre-action behaviour.

- If proceedings have been served and negotiations are likely, consider an application on paper for an agreed stay.

- Consider mediation (and the costs consequences of refusing a request for mediation) and other forms of ADR.

- Attempt to agree directions with the opposing party and submit draft directions to the court in good time, flagging any differences between the parties to the judge to assist with case management. Some County Court Hearing Centres (for example, Central London) have their own proposed model directions.

- Have an eye at all times to costs. Consider early voluntary disclosure (if you have a strong case and there are no hostages to fortune) to build pressure on the other side. Consider making an appropriate offer to settle for similar reasons.

CHAPTER TWENTY-FOUR
CONCLUSION: THE FUTURE OF THE LTA 1954

In the leading case of *O'May v City of London Real Property Co. Ltd* [1983] 2 AC 726, Lord Hailsham described the general purpose of the 1954 Act at 740 as being '*to protect the business interests of the tenant so far as they are affected by the approaching termination of the current lease, in particular as regards his security of tenure*'. Lord Sumption in *S Franses Ltd v Cavendish Hotel (London) Ltd* [2018] UKSC 62, [2019] AC 249 observed at [16], however, that the LTA 1954 "*confers no more than a qualified security on the tenant. Certain interests of the landlord override whatever security it was intended to confer on the tenant, and one of them is the right to demolish or reconstruct his property in whatever way he chooses at the expiry of the term.*" This book has depicted the practical operation of this balancing exercise between landlord and tenant.

The LTA 1954 has been periodically reviewed and amended. Two Law Commission reports into the LTA 1954 have been published, in 1969 and 1992, resulting in the changes made by the Law of Property Act 1969 and the Regulatory Reforms (Business Tenancies) (England and Wales) Order 2003. Overall, however, the balance between the landlord and the tenant has been left the same. The system of statutory continuation, landlord and tenant notices, and court-based determination of any opposition to renewal of the tenancy remains substantially the same.

The LTA 1954 is a familiar piece of legislation. It has been well-explored with only a few exceptions (ground D being one). The history of its predecessors is not such a picture of stability. As Michael Haley describes in his article, 'The statutory regulation of business tenancies: private property, public interest and political compromise' (1999) Legal Studies 19(2) 207, there had been proposals for legislation to protect business tenants from exploitation as early as 1899. In the post-First World War economy, these problems refused to go away, leading to a succession of Bills which were blocked by the government of the day. The Landlord and Tenant Act 1927 failed, however, to introduce security of tenure as a direct right, affording little protection in most cases. These difficulties were exacerbated post-1945. Interim legislation, the Leasehold Property (Temporary Provisions) Act 1951 introduced a limited right to statutory renewal of business tenancies. In 1953, a White Paper entitled 'Government Policy on Leasehold Property in England and Wales' accepted the case for improved security of tenure. This led to Part II of the Landlord and Tenant Bill introduced before Parliament in December 1953. Part II was generally uncontroversial, and on 1 October 1954, the LTA 1954 came into force.

Subject to the limited modifications introduced by the Law of Property Act 1969 and then the 2003 Order, the statutory scheme and overall balance of Part II of the LTA 1954 has remained unaltered. This situation which should be contrasted with the radical changes in business leasehold tenure between 1925 and 1955. Cynically, it might be argued that this is because many business leases are contracted out of the LTA 1954. The LTA 1954 remains prominent, however: it has not suffered the same apathy and disuse as Part I of the Landlord and Tenant Act 1927 (dealing with compensation for improvements). The Law Commission recommended its abolition in 1989, but such has been the limited impact of Part I of the 1927 Act that this created no waves and it lingers on in force.

The Law Commission periodically reviews the LTA 1954. It actively declined to re-visit the LTA 1954 in the 13th Programme of Law Reform. Once again, there are some calls for the Act to be abolished (most notably by David Neuberger: 'Our Not So Flexible Friend' (2000) 39 EG139), but this is very unlikely. Instead, it is more likely that we shall see more technical changes to problematic aspects of the LTA 1954. The British Property Federation, for example, has recommended simplifying the current 'contracting out' provisions, fixing the commencement date of a renewal lease to a predictable date and consequently fixing the valuation date for all renewal leases, and the referral of disputes over renewal rent to a valuation specialist rather than a Judge in the County Court. These are all sensible and modest proposals, which reflect the fact that it is often the renewal rent that leads parties into dispute.

In 2015, Professor Mark Pawlowski and Dr James Brown carried out an extensive questionnaire survey of legal and surveying professionals. The results of their study were published in two parts in the Landlord and

Tenant Review: L&T Review 2015, 19(4), 162-166, L. & T. Review 2015, 19(5), 185-189. The survey identified a need to further simplify the contracting out procedure. They also argued that the LTA 1954 would benefit from further amendments to the rules on interim rents. On the whole, however, their conclusion was that the LTA 1954 was working well.

Practitioners, therefore, should not expect the LTA 1954 to be either abolished or radically recast in the near future. The excitement created by the *Franses* case in December 2018 did not translate into a significant change in how Ground F cases are dealt with in practice, save for a more focussed inquiry into the landlord's intent behind each project. The fact that this Second Edition has not required a significant re-working of the First Edition is witness to the overall stability of the operation of Part II of the LTA 1954.

Further simplification of the LTA 1954 would, indeed, be a practical and welcome aspiration for the Law Commission. In particular, both the statutory machinery and the court procedure for the determination of interim rent is overly complicated: as a result, such issues are typically postponed until the final hearing of the application, which rather defeats much of the purpose of the provisions. In practice, the Pilot Scheme at the County Court at Central London has been a success: it remains to be seen if it will be extended both in geographic reach and to opposed lease renewals.

Until then, the authors of this book hope that this work has, in a small way, made the workings of the LTA 1954 more accessible for the reader in practice.

APPENDIX
NOTICES UNDER THE LANDLORD AND TENANT ACT 1954

Prescribed notices

The Landlord and Tenant Act 1954, Part 2 (Notices) Regulations 2004 (SI 2004/1005) ('the Notices Regs') prescribe a number of the most important forms which should be used under the LTA 1954. Instead of re-printing the Notices Regs, a list of the most important forms is recited below, along with their corresponding form number. You should have regard to Schedule 1 of the Notices Regs, which definitively sets out the purpose for each prescribed form. Not all of the prescribed forms are listed below – in particular, there are a number of forms which only apply where there are residential parts which might potentially engage the Leasehold Reform Act 1967 – you should consider Schedule 1 to determine which form best fits the situation.

Section 25 notices

- Non-hostile section 25 notice: Form 1.

- Hostile section 25 notice, tenant not entitled under the Leasehold Reform Act 1967 to buy the freehold or an extended lease: Form 2.

- Hostile section 25 notice where the tenant may be entitled under the Leasehold Reform Act 1967 to buy the freehold or an extended lease (notice under section 25 LTA 1954 and paragraph 10 of Schedule 3 LRA 1967): Form 7.

- Withdrawal of section 25 notice under section 44 and paragraph 6 of Schedule 6 LTA 1954: Form 6.

<u>Section 26 notices</u>

- Section 26 notice: Form 3.

<u>Section 40 notices</u>

- Landlord's section 40 notice to tenant to provide information: Form 4.

- Tenant's section 40 notice to reversioner or reversioner's mortgagee to provide information: Form 6.

<u>Notices for which no form is prescribed</u>

There are some provisions which require a notice under the LTA 1954 but for which no form is prescribed by the Notice Regs. As with any precedent, the following should be considered critically and adapted to fit the case that you are dealing with.

Tenant's notice to terminate under LTA 1954 section 27(1)

To: [NAME OF IMMEDIATE LANDLORD] of [ADDRESS] (Landlord).

From: [NAME OF TENANT] of [ADDRESS] (Tenant).

Regarding the premises: [ADDRESS OF PROPERTY] (Property).

The Tenant is the tenant of the Property and you are the Landlord by virtue of a lease dated [DATE] and made between [NAMES OF ORIGINAL PARTIES TO THE LEASE] (Lease). The Lease will expire on [termination date]. The Tenant does not desire the Tenancy to continue past this date under the provisions of Part II of the Landlord and Tenant Act 1954.

[I or WE], [TENANT] give you notice under section 27(1) of the Landlord and Tenant Act 1954.

Dated:

SIGNED: ....

The tenant

Tenant's notice to terminate under LTA 1954 section 27(2)

To: [NAME OF IMMEDIATE LANDLORD] of [ADDRESS] (Landlord).

From: [NAME OF TENANT] of [ADDRESS] (Tenant).

Regarding the premises: [ADDRESS OF PROPERTY] (Property).

The Tenant is the tenant of the Property and you are the Landlord by virtue of a lease dated [DATE] and made between [NAMES OF ORIGINAL PARTIES TO THE LEASE] (Lease). [The Lease expired on [termination date] / The Lease will expire on [termination date](delete as appropriate)] at which point the lease [continues / will continue] under section 24 of the Landlord and Tenant Act 1954.

[I or WE], [TENANT] give you notice under section 27(2) of the Landlord and Tenant Act 1954 that the tenancy will be brought to an end on [date tenancy to end] by virtue of this notice.

Dated:

SIGNED: ....

The tenant

Landlord's notice under section 24(3)(a) of the LTA 1954

To: [NAME OF TENANT] of [ADDRESS] (Tenant).

From: [NAME OF LANDLORD] of [ADDRESS] (Landlord).

Regarding the premises: [ADDRESS OF PROPERTY] (Property).

I give you notice under the Landlord and Tenant Act 1954 section 24(3)(a) that Part II of the Landlord and Tenant Act 1954 has ceased to apply to your tenancy of the above premises. Your tenancy will terminate by virtue of this notice on [date of termination].

Dated:

Signed:

The Landlord

Landlord's response to tenant's section 26 notice

To: [NAME OF TENANT] of [ADDRESS] (Tenant).

From: [NAME OF LANDLORD] of [ADDRESS] (Landlord).

Regarding the premises: [ADDRESS OF PROPERTY] (Property).

I have received your request for a new tenancy of the above premises dated [date of tenant's request]) given under the Landlord and Tenant Act 1954 Section 26. I give you notice that I will oppose an application to the court for the grant of a new tenancy on the ground[s] set out in paragraph[s] [insert relevant paragraph number or numbers of grounds under section 30(1)] of Section 30(1) of the Landlord and Tenant Act 1954.

Dated:

Signed:

The Landlord

MORE BOOKS BY LAW BRIEF PUBLISHING

A selection of our other titles available now:-

'Covid-19, Homeworking and the Law – The Essential Guide to Employment and GDPR Issues' by Forbes Solicitors

'Covid-19, Force Majeure and Frustration of Contracts – The Essential Guide' by Keith Markham

'Covid-19 and Criminal Law – The Essential Guide' by Ramya Nagesh

'Covid-19 and Family Law in England and Wales – The Essential Guide' by Safda Mahmood

'A Practical Guide to the Law of Unlawful Eviction and Harassment – 2nd Edition' by Stephanie Lovegrove

'Covid-19, Residential Property, Equity Release and Enfranchisement – The Essential Guide' by Paul Sams and Louise Uphill

'Covid-19, Brexit and the Law of Commercial Leases – The Essential Guide' by Mark Shelton

'A Practical Guide to Costs in Personal Injury Claims – 2nd Edition' by Matthew Hoe

'A Practical Guide to the General Data Protection Regulation (GDPR) – 2nd Edition' by Keith Markham

'Ellis on Credit Hire – Sixth Edition' by Aidan Ellis & Tim Kevan

'A Practical Guide to Working with Litigants in Person and McKenzie Friends in Family Cases' by Stuart Barlow

'Protecting Unregistered Brands: A Practical Guide to the Law of Passing Off' by Lorna Brazell

'A Practical Guide to Secondary Liability and Joint Enterprise Post-Jogee' by Joanne Cecil & James Mehigan

'A Practical Guide to the Pre-Action RTA Claims Protocol for Personal Injury Lawyers' by Antonia Ford

'A Practical Guide to Neighbour Disputes and the Law' by Alexander Walsh

'A Practical Guide to Forfeiture of Leases' by Mark Shelton

'A Practical Guide to Coercive Control for Legal Practitioners and Victims' by Rachel Horman

'A Practical Guide to Rights Over Airspace and Subsoil' by Daniel Gatty
'Tackling Disclosure in the Criminal Courts – A Practitioner's Guide' by Narita Bahra QC & Don Ramble
'A Practical Guide to the Law of Driverless Cars – Second Edition' by Alex Glassbrook, Emma Northey & Scarlett Milligan
'A Practical Guide to TOLATA Claims' by Greg Williams
'Artificial Intelligence – The Practical Legal Issues' by John Buyers
'A Practical Guide to the Law of Prescription in Scotland' by Andrew Foyle
'A Practical Guide to the Construction and Rectification of Wills and Trust Instruments' by Edward Hewitt
'A Practical Guide to the Law of Bullying and Harassment in the Workplace' by Philip Hyland
'How to Be a Freelance Solicitor: A Practical Guide to the SRA-Regulated Freelance Solicitor Model' by Paul Bennett
'A Practical Guide to Prison Injury Claims' by Malcolm Johnson
'A Practical Guide to the Small Claims Track' by Dominic Bright
'A Practical Guide to Advising Clients at the Police Station' by Colin Stephen McKeown-Beaumont
'A Practical Guide to Antisocial Behaviour Injunctions' by Iain Wightwick
'Practical Mediation: A Guide for Mediators, Advocates, Advisers, Lawyers, and Students in Civil, Commercial, Business, Property, Workplace, and Employment Cases' by Jonathan Dingle with John Sephton
'The Mini-Pupillage Workbook' by David Boyle
'A Practical Guide to Crofting Law' by Brian Inkster
'A Practical Guide to Spousal Maintenance' by Liz Cowell
'A Practical Guide to the Law of Domain Names and Cybersquatting' by Andrew Clemson
'A Practical Guide to the Law of Gender Pay Gap Reporting' by Harini Iyengar

'A Practical Guide to the Rights of Grandparents in Children Proceedings' by Stuart Barlow
'NHS Whistleblowing and the Law' by Joseph England
'Employment Law and the Gig Economy' by Nigel Mackay & Annie Powell
'A Practical Guide to Noise Induced Hearing Loss (NIHL) Claims' by Andrew Mckie, Ian Skeate, Gareth McAloon
'An Introduction to Beauty Negligence Claims – A Practical Guide for the Personal Injury Practitioner' by Greg Almond
'Intercompany Agreements for Transfer Pricing Compliance' by Paul Sutton
'Zen and the Art of Mediation' by Martin Plowman
'A Practical Guide to the SRA Principles, Individual and Law Firm Codes of Conduct 2019 – What Every Law Firm Needs to Know' by Paul Bennett
'A Practical Guide to Adoption for Family Lawyers' by Graham Pegg
'A Practical Guide to Industrial Disease Claims' by Andrew Mckie & Ian Skeate
'A Practical Guide to Redundancy' by Philip Hyland
'A Practical Guide to Vicarious Liability' by Mariel Irvine
'A Practical Guide to Applications for Landlord's Consent and Variation of Leases' by Mark Shelton
'A Practical Guide to Relief from Sanctions Post-Mitchell and Denton' by Peter Causton
'A Practical Guide to Equity Release for Advisors' by Paul Sams
'A Practical Guide to the Law Relating to Food' by Ian Thomas
'A Practical Guide to Financial Services Claims' by Chris Hegarty
'The Law of Houses in Multiple Occupation: A Practical Guide to HMO Proceedings' by Julian Hunt
'A Practical Guide to Unlawful Eviction and Harassment' by Stephanie Lovegrove
'Occupiers, Highways and Defective Premises Claims: A Practical Guide Post-Jackson – 2nd Edition' by Andrew Mckie

'A Practical Guide to Financial Ombudsman Service Claims' by Adam Temple & Robert Scrivenor
'A Practical Guide to Advising Schools on Employment Law' by Jonathan Holden
'A Practical Guide to Running Housing Disrepair and Cavity Wall Claims: 2nd Edition' by Andrew Mckie & Ian Skeate
'A Practical Guide to Holiday Sickness Claims – 2nd Edition' by Andrew Mckie & Ian Skeate
'Arguments and Tactics for Personal Injury and Clinical Negligence Claims' by Dorian Williams
'A Practical Guide to Drone Law' by Rufus Ballaster, Andrew Firman, Eleanor Clot
'A Practical Guide to Compliance for Personal Injury Firms Working With Claims Management Companies' by Paul Bennett
'A Practical Guide to Dog Law for Owners and Others' by Andrea Pitt
'RTA Allegations of Fraud in a Post-Jackson Era: The Handbook – 2nd Edition' by Andrew Mckie
'RTA Personal Injury Claims: A Practical Guide Post-Jackson' by Andrew Mckie
'On Experts: CPR35 for Lawyers and Experts' by David Boyle
'An Introduction to Personal Injury Law' by David Boyle
'A Practical Guide to Subtle Brain Injury Claims' by Pankaj Madan

These books and more are available to order online direct from the publisher at www.lawbriefpublishing.com, where you can also read free sample chapters. For any queries, contact us on 0844 587 2383 or mail@lawbriefpublishing.com.

Our books are also usually in stock at www.amazon.co.uk with free next day delivery for Prime members, and at good legal bookshops such as Wildy & Sons.

We are regularly launching new books in our series of practical day-to-day practitioners' guides. Visit our website and join our free newsletter to be kept informed and to receive special offers, free chapters, etc.

You can also follow us on Twitter at www.twitter.com/lawbriefpub.

www.ingramcontent.com/pod-product-compliance
Lightning Source LLC
LaVergne TN
LVHW052320200926
848481LV00002B/622